St. Ambrose
On Repentance

St. Ambrose
On Repentance

St. Ambrose
On Repentance

© Lighthouse Publishing 2013

Published by
Lighthouse Christian Publishing
SAN 257-4330
5531 Dufferin Drive
Savage, Minnesota, 55378
United States of America

www.lighthousechristianpublishing.com

ON THE DOCTRINE OF ST. AMBROSE

There is a very complete agreement on the part of St. Ambrose with the Catholic teaching of the universal Church. St. Augustine speaks of him as "a faithful teacher of the Church, and even at the risk of his life a most strenuous defender of Catholic truth,"[2] "whose skill, constancy, labors, and perils, both on account of what he did and what he wrote, the Roman world unhesitatingly proclaims." In matters both of faith and morals by his words and writings he greatly benefited the Church and was called by St. Jerome "a pillar of the Church."

In his dogmatic treatises, more particularly in his books on the Faith, he shows great skill and penetration, and his reasoning is full and clear, meeting the most subtle objections with patient industry. Scarcely any ancient writer has treated the mystery of the Holy Trinity and the theological difficulties connected with it more clearly and convincingly than St. Ambrose in his *De Fide* and *De Spiritu Sancto.*

In his expositions of Holy Scripture he treats of the threefold sense, the literal, the moral, and the mystical, devoting more pains, however, and time to the latter than to the former. He gives special consideration to the mystical interpretation of such passages as may seem to contain in a literal sense anything diverging from sound morality. Many of his other mystical interpretations of plain, simple matters of fact have much beauty, as in his treatment of the story of the building of the ark, the marriage of Isaac, and the blessings of the Patriarchs. The literal sense is followed specially in the *Hexaëmeron*, the treatise on Paradise, Noah and the Ark, and the Exposition of the Gospel according to St. Luke. The moral sense, though referred to throughout his writings, is more particularly sought out in the Expositions of the Psalms.

St. Ambrose was a diligent student of the Greek writers, whom he often follows largely, especially Origen and Didymus, as also St. Basil the Great and St. Athanasius, and he has also adapted many points of allegorical interpretation from Philo. He is fond of alleging scriptural proofs, and when he argues from reason often confirms his argument by some quotation or reference, a task easy for him who, from his consecration, was so diligent a student of Holy Scripture.

As to justification, St. Ambrose ascribes the whole work to the Holy Spirit, Who seals us in our hearts, as we receive the outward sign in our bodies. Through the Holy Spirit we receive a share of the grace of adoption. Christ was perfect according to the fullness of His Majesty; we are perfected by a continual progress in virtue.

With regard to baptism, he taught in accordance with the received belief of his day that it is the sacrament of adoption and regeneration, wherein sin is forgiven,6 and the Holy Spirit confers new life upon the soul and joins it mystically to Christ. As to the Real Presence in the Sacrament of the Eucharist, his doctrine is no less definite. In his treatise on the Faith he says of the elements that they "are transfigured by the mystery of the sacred prayer into flesh and blood." He interprets various texts, also, in many places in the same sense. In a like spirit he maintains that the power of forgiving sins on repentance is vested in the ministry of the Church.9 The intercession of the saints, and up to a certain point their invocation, is likewise upheld.

There was a Latin version made from the Septuagint, including the Apocrypha, in Africa, and in use there at the end of the second century, very barbarous, and copying even Greek constructions. Of this text SS. Ambrose and Augustine used a recension. But our author seems to have been very independent, and to have made use of several different versions of holy Scripture, translating, as it would seem, often for himself from the Septuagint, referring also to Symmachus, Theodotion, and Aquila, though thinking less of the latter. When the prophets, he says, were moved by the Holy Spirit, they were troubled and darkened with their own ignorance. Prayer, he asserts, is necessary for understanding holy Scripture. Each Testament is not equally easy, and we are not to criticize

what we do not understand.13 He speaks of the Hebrew as the truth,14 but states that the Septuagint added much that is useful.

The Arians are repeatedly charged by St. Ambrose with falsifying and manipulating Scripture for their own ends, not always, it would seem, very justly, but the same charge is a common one against all heretical bodies in early days. As to the Canon, he would seem to have no very definite rule. He admits Tobit as prophetic, Judith as canonical, nor does he distinguish between canonical and deuterocanonical, while the sapiential books are all attributed to Solomon. He quotes Baruch as Jeremiah, and refers to the History of Susanna, Bel and the Dragon, and other apocryphal works as "Scripture." Ezra, he says, re-established Holy Scripture by memory, and he quotes the fourth book of Esdras.

LIFE OF ST. AMBROSE

St. Ambrose, Bishop of Milan, one of the four Latin
doctors of the Church, was descended from a Roman
family of some distinction, some time Christian, and
counting martyrs as well as state officials amongst its
members.

His father, likewise named Ambrosius, was prefect of the
Gauls, an office the jurisdiction of which extended over
Spain, Britain, Cis- and Trans-Alpine Gaul. His chief
official residence was Trèves, where probably St.
Ambrose was born, as seems most likely, A.D. 340.

After his father's death, his mother and his elder brother,
Satyrus, went with St. Ambrose to Rome, not earlier than
353, where his elder sister, Marcellina, received the veil at
Christmas from Pope Liberius, the exact year being
uncertain.

Here the future bishop devoted himself to legal studies, in which he met with great success. His skill in law and general reputation soon led to his advancement, and about A.D. 370 he was appointed by the Prætorian Prefect Probus governor of Liguria and Æmilia, with the rank of consular. On this occasion Probus is said to have closed an address to St. Ambrose with the words, "Go and act, not as a judge, but as a bishop." This advice was so well followed by Ambrose, that owing to his equity and kindness the people came to look up to him rather as a father than as a judge.

After some few years Auxentius, the intended Arian Bishop of Milan, died, A.D. 374, and it is said that during the discussion as to the appointment of his successor a child cried out in the assembly, "Ambrose Bishop," and, although he was but a catechumen and so canonically unqualified, the multitude immediately elected him by acclamation.

St. Ambrose did all in his power, even, if we accept the statements if his biographer Paulinus, probably a clerk of Milan, resorting to some questionable expedients, to escape from the dignity laid upon him, but when his election was ratified by the Emperor Valentinian, he recognized his appointment as being the will of God, and insisted on being baptized by a Catholic priest. Eight days later, December 7, A.D. 374, he was consecrated Bishop.

The first care of the new bishop was at once to divest himself of his worldly property, giving his silver and gold to the poor and the Church, and committing the management of his estates, except a life interest for his sister, to his brother Satyrus, who gave up his own office to come to his assistance, and enable him to devote himself wholly to theological study and his other Episcopal duties.

His chief studies were Holy Scripture and ecclesiastical writers, especially St. Basil the Great and Didymus of Alexandria, from whom no less a man than St. Jerome accused him of plagiarizing. His natural abilities and thorough knowledge of Greek stood him in good stead, when, as he says himself, he had to learn and to teach at the same time.

The life of St. Ambrose was a pattern of the discharge of episcopal duties. He spent much time daily in study and devotion, besides the more public duties of his office. He preached every Sunday and at certain seasons daily. His labours in preparing catechumens for baptism were blessed with great success, amongst those taught by him being St. Augustine.

But the zeal and courage of the new Bishop were soon tried. The Empress mother Justina was still an Arian, but had little influence during the life of the Emperor Gratian, who was much attached to St. Ambrose. After his murder, however, A.D. 383, his brother Valentinian II., a boy of only twelve years of age, ascended the throne and was naturally much under his mother's influence. Justina led him to support a demand of the Arians for the use of the Portian basilica, situated outside the walls of Milan. This being refused, a second application was made for the large and newer basilica within the city. Ambrose replied, "The Emperor has his palaces, let him leave the churches to the Bishop." Soldiers were sent to secure the delivery of the basilica, but St. Ambrose with the faithful occupied the building and remained within, singing psalms and hymns till the soldiers retired.

St. Ambrose was no less successful in his zeal against the expiring heathenism of Italy than against Arianism. One of the many remnants till recent times of heathen worship had been the Altar of Victory in the Senate-house at Rome, which was removed under Gratian; the prefect of Rome, Symmachus, himself a heathen but a friend of St. Ambrose, appealed to Valentinan II. that it might be restored, and Ambrose successfully opposed this appeal in two Epistles (17, 18) addressed to the young Emperor. Yet again, when Theodosius assumed the imperial power [A.D. 387], a renewed attempt was made and once more frustrated. Later on, Eugenius the usurper judged it politic to take the heathen's side, the Altar of Victory was once more set up, and the temples stood open as in the days of old. But this triumph lasted only for a brief period. When Theodosius defeated the usurper at Aquileia, in the spring of 394, he also defeated paganism, which sank to rise no more as a public religion, though it long lingered in private amidst indifference, toleration, and at times persecution.

The influence exercised by Ambrose upon the rulers of his day is sufficiently manifested by these facts, but he had the courage to use not only influence, but, when needed, rebuke and Church discipline.

Only a few months after his elevation to the see of Milan, he remonstrated with Valentinian I. concerning the severity of his rule and other abuses, and required amendment. The Emperor's reply did him honor: "Well, if I have offended, prescribe for me the remedies which the law of God requires." Again, on another occasion, in 390, Theodosius had put down a seditious movement in Thessalonica with great severity, causing some 7,000 persons to be slain. St. Ambrose at once, disregarding the possible consequences to himself, wrote him a letter (Ep. 51) on the subject, exhorting him to repentance, and pointing out that he could not permit him to be present at the celebration of the Mysteries, till he had openly testified his sorrow. At another time when the same Emperor had ventured into the sanctuary or chancel of the church, which was the right of the clergy alone, St. Ambrose rebuked him and caused him to retire.

These acts of ecclesiastical discipline were also accompanied by others in which the great Bishop was able in temporal matters to assist the imperial family.

Twice on behalf of the young Emperor Valentinian II. he undertook a mission to Trèves, to see the usurper Maximus, and when Valentinian died, St. Ambrose delivered a striking oration at his funeral, recording his many virtues. Theodosius did not survive his victory over Eugenius for many months. In January of the following year [A.D. 395], he died at Milan, and the funeral oration which St. Ambrose pronounced over him is also extant.

Yet whilst thus devoting much time to weighty affairs of State, the Bishop never neglected the duties of his office. He preached every Sunday, at great festivals, once or more often, every day. He celebrated the Holy Mysteries daily. His life was marked by perfect purity, sympathy, energy, and devotion. He was always ready to help those requiring assistance, and so when Augustine came to Milan to teach rhetoric, A.D. 384, he was kindly received and fascinated. Probably he owed his conversion even more to the life and character than to the teaching of St. Ambrose.

One subject St. Ambrose never tired of recommending was Virginity; and such was the power of his exhortations that mothers used to forbid their daughters to attend his sermons and addresses.

The indefatigable zeal of the great Bishop further exhibited itself in the number of his writings. Many of them consist of addresses subsequently worked up into treatises, and are on all subjects, dogmatic, controversial, exegetical, and ascetic. There remain also a large number of valuable letters, and some hymns, probably from four to twelve of those ascribed to him being genuine, and in use to the present day.

But besides his writings and his resistance to the attacks of Arianism, heathenism, or the secular power, St. Ambrose devoted himself to actively defending the cause of the Church and of orthodoxy wherever he had the opportunity. Although the death of Satyrus, A.D. 379, must have greatly added to the troubles of St. Ambrose, he was as watchful as ever against all possibilities of heretical aggression. To his care and opposition to the party of the Empress Justina it was owing that the city of Sirmium was preserved in A.D. 381 from receiving an Arian bishop. And in the same year, when the Arians, hoping for large

support from the East, had almost persuaded the Emperor
to summon a general council at Aquileia, St. Ambrose
prevailed upon him to summon only the neighbouring
bishops, and what might have been a serious evil was
avoided.

In such ways the holy man, embracing in his far-seeing
care the interests of religion far and wide, spent his days
in uneasing labour till his health failed in the year 397,
when, as is related by Paulinus, Count Stilicho, saying
that the loss of such a man threatened destruction to Italy,
persuaded the nobles of the city to request St. Ambrose
that he would pray for longer life. But the Saint replied:
"I have not so lived amongst you as to be ashamed of
living, and I do not fear to die, for we have a good Lord."
As some of the bystanders were discussing in whispers
who would be St. Ambrose's successor, and mentioned
Simplicianus, he overheard them, and said, "An old man,
but good." For the last few hours of his life Ambrose lay
with his arms extended in the form of a cross, praying.
Honoratus, Bishop of Vercellæ, lying in another room,
heard himself called thrice, and coming down, offered
him the Body of the Lord, after receiving which St.
Ambrose breathed his last, on Good Friday night, April
4–5, A.D. 397, and was laid to rest on Easter morning in
the Ambrosian basilica at Milan, where he still is
reverenced, and in which the Ambrosian liturgy and rites,
differing considerably from the Roman use of the rest of
the churches of Italy, continue to this day, though
doubtless with many modifications subsequent to the time
of St. Ambrose.

WRITINGS OF ST. AMBROSE

The extant writings of St. Ambrose may be divided under six heads. I. Dogmatic; II. Exegetic; III. Moral; IV. Sermons; V. Letters; VI. A few Hymns.

I. DOGMATIC AND CONTROVERSIAL WORKS.

1. *De Fide.* The chief of these are the Five Books on the Faith, of which the two first were written in compliance with a request of the Emperor Gratian, A.D. 378. Books III.–V. were written in 379 or 380, and seem to have been worked up from addresses delivered to the people [V. prol. 9, 11; III. 143; IV. 119]. This treatise vindicates the Divinity of Christ from the attacks of the Arians, and has always enjoyed the highest reputation, being quoted and referred to again and again.

2. *De Spiritu Sancto.* The three books on the Holy Spirit may be considered as a continuation of the above treatise, and were also addressed to Gratian in compliance with his

request, A.D. 381. In this treatise St. Ambrose shows that the Holy Spirit is God, and of one nature and substance with the Father and the Son. He makes use of the Greek writers, SS. Didymus, Basil the Great, and Athanasius, and was on this ground attacked by St. Jerome. See Rufinus, *Apol. adv. Hieron.* II. 23–25.

3. *De Incarnationis Dominicæ Sacramento.* The book on the Mystery of the Lord's Incarnation owed its origin to a challenge to dispute publicly given to St. Ambrose by two Arian chamberlains of Gratian. On the day appointed they were, as Paulinus relates in his life of St. Ambrose, thrown out of the chariot which was conveying them and killed. On the next day, that the people might not be disappointed, this discourse was delivered, but the reference made to the absence of the challengers hardly suits the story of Paulinus. The treatise is a very valuable argument in defence of our Lord's Divinity and Eternity, and that He is perfect God and perfect Man. In rewriting the address the Bishop added a refutation of the argument that the Begotten and the Unbegotten could not be of one nature and substance. The treatise may be considered as a supplement to that concerning the Faith.

4. *De Mysteriis.* A valuable treatise on the Mysteries, under which title St. Ambrose includes Baptism, with its complement, Confirmation, and the Eucharist. It is somewhat similar to the *Catecheses Mystagogicæ* of St. Cyril of Jerusalem, expounding the doctrine and ceremonies of these sacraments. On doctrinal grounds the authenticity of the work has been impugned by some modern writers, but there is no sufficient foundation for their arguments, as the teaching may be paralleled in

many other passages of St. Ambrose. The date is not certain, but may be about A.D. 387.

5. *Libri duo de poenitentia.* These books on Penitence were written about A.D. 384, against the Novatians. In the first book the writer proves that the power of forgiving sins was left by Christ to His Church. In the second book, insisting on the necessity of repentance and confession, he also refutes the Novatian interpretations of Heb. vi. 4–6 and St. Matt. xii. 31–32. This treatise has also undeservedly been questioned on doctrinal grounds by some moderns. These treatises are all translated in this volume.

II. EXEGETICAL WORKS.

St. Ambrose was in the habit of explaining various books of holy Scripture in courses of lectures, which he subsequently worked up, often at the request of friends, into treatises in the shape in which they have come down to us. Of the class we have:

1. *Hexaëmeron.* This treatise, expounding the literal and moral sense of the work of the six days of creation [Gen. i. 1–26], consists of nine addresses to the people of Milan, delivered in the last week of Lent, probably A.D. 389, and is now divided into six books. The writer has studied Origen, but followed rather the teaching of St. Hippolytus and Basil the Great, though he expresses himself often quite in a different sense.

2. *De Paradiso.* This is the earliest or one of the earliest of the extant writings of St. Ambrose, though the exact

date is uncertain. In it he discusses what and where Paradise was, and the question of the life of our first parents there, the temptation, fall and its results, and answers certain cavils of the Gnostics and Manichees. He also enters into an allegorical exposition comparing Paradise with the human soul.

3. *De Cain et Abel.* The treatise is now divided into two books, but the division is too inartistic to have been made by the writer. As to the date, it was later than the last treatise, but probably not many months. The interpretations are very mystical, and touch upon moral and dogmatic questions.

4. *De Noe et Arca.* This treatise has reached us in a mutilated condition. It was written probably before the *De Officiis* and *De Abraham,* but after the works on Paradise and Cain and Abel, though the exact date cannot be determined. The exposition is literal and allegorical.

5. *De Patriarchis.* Seven books preached and written at various dates about 387 or 388. The same kind of interpretation is followed in these as in the former treatises.

6. *De fuga sæculi.* Written probably about A.D. 389–390. An instructive treatise setting forth the desirability of avoiding the dangers of the world, and for those who must live in the world, showing how to pass through them most safely.

7. *De Elia et jejunio.* A treatise composed from addresses delivered during Lent, certainly after A.D. 386, possibly 389.

8. *De Tobia.* A work quoted by St. Augustine (*C. Jul. Pelag.* I. 3, 10), consisting of sermons on the story of Tobias, and chiefly directed against the practice of usury.

9. *De Nabuthe Jezraelita.* One or two sermons against avarice, probably written about A.D. 395.

10. *Libri* iv. *de interpellatione Job et David.* The first and third books have Job, the second and fourth David, for their subject, and formed a course of sermons the date of which is uncertain.

11. *Apologia prophetæ David ad Theodosium Augustum.* A number of addresses delivered, it would seem, about A.D. 384, quoted also by St. Augustine.

12. *Enarrationes in* xii. *Psalmos Davidicos.* Commentaries on Psalms 1, 35–40, 43, 45, 47, 48, 61 (according to St. Ambrose's numbering). These seem to have been partly preached, partly dictated at various dates, and much in them is borrowed from St. Basil.

13. *Expositio Psalmi* cxviii. This treatise is one of the most carefully worked out of all the writings of St. Ambrose and consists of twenty-two addresses to the faithful, each address comprising one division of the Psalm. From various allusions, it would seem that the completed work dates from about A.D. 388.

14. *Expositio Evangelii secundum Lucam.* The ten books of this commentary consist likewise of sermons in which St. Ambrose explained the Gospel during a period of one or two years, in 386

III. Ethical Writings.

Among the ethical or moral writings of St. Ambrose, the first place is deservedly assigned to:

1. *De Officiis Ministrorum.* In three books, which are translated in this series.

2. *De Virginibus.* Three books concerning Virgins, addressed to his sister Marcellina in the year 377, probably, like most of the treatises of St. Ambrose, revised from addresses, the first of which was delivered on the festival of St. Agnes, January 21. This would seem to have been perhaps the very earliest of the writings of St. Ambrose, judging from the opening chapter. The treatise is referred to by St. Jerome, St. Augustine, Cassian, and others.

3. *De Viduis.* This shorter work, concerning Widows, was probably written not very long after the last mentioned treatise.

4. *De Virginitate.* A treatise on Virginity, the date of which cannot certainly be fixed, but the writing *De Viduis* is referred to in chapter 9.

5. *De Institutione Virginis.* A treatise on the training and discipline of a Virgin, addressed to Eusebius, either

bishop or a noble of Bologna, after St. Ambrose had admitted his niece to the rank of Virgins, probably about A.D. 391 or 392.

6. *Exhortatio Virginitatis.* A commendation of Virginity preached on the occasion of the consecration of a church at Florence by St. Ambrose, A.D. 393 or 394.

IV. SERMONS AND ADDRESSES.

1. *Contra Auxentium.* A sermon against Auxentius, concerning giving up the basilicas to the Arians, usually inserted between the twenty-first and twenty-second of the letters of St. Ambrose.

2. *De Excessu fratris Satyri.* The two addresses on the occasion of the death of St. Ambrose's brother Satyrus, translated in this volume.

3. *De obitu Valentiniani Consolatio.* The Emperor Valentinian having been murdered by Arbogastes, Count of Vienne, his body was brought to Milan, and remained two months unburied. At last Theodosius sent the necessary rescript, and at the funeral solemnities St. Ambrose delivered the address entitled the "Consolation."

4. *De obitu Theodosii oratio.* A discourse delivered forty days after the death of the Emperor Theodosius before the Emperor Honorius at Milan.

V. THE LETTERS OF ST. AMBROSE.

The Benedictine Editors of St. Ambrose have divided his Epistles into two classes: the first comprising those to which they thought it possible to assign dates; the second those which afford no data for a conclusion. Probably in many cases the exact year is not so certain as the editors have made it appear, but they seem arranged in a fairly probable consecutive order.

THE LETTERS

1. To the Emperor Gratian, in reply to his request for a treatise on the Faith. Written A.D. 379, before August, as Gratian came to Milan in that month.

2. To Constantius, a bishop, on episcopal duties, and commending to him the care of the vacant see of Forum Cornelii, or Imola. Probably written about A.D. 379.

3, 4. To Cornelius, Bishop of Comum, the first a friendly letter, the second containing also an invitation to the consecration of a church by Bassianus, Bishop of Laus Pompeia, now Lodi Vecchio, near Milan. Written probably after A.D. 381.

5, 6. To Syagrius, Bishop of Verona. On a charge falsely brought against the Virgin Indicia. They may have been written A.D. 380.

7, 8. To Justus, perhaps Bishop of Lyons. On Holy Scripture. If the conjecture that Justus was the Bishop of Lyons is correct, written about 380 or 381.

9–12. Letters concerning the Council of Aquileia, held A.D. 381, to the bishops of the provinces of Gaul, to the Emperor Gratian and his colleagues. Two men, Palladius and Secundianus, held Arian opinions, and the former appears to have asked Gratian to convoke a General Council, pleading that he was unjustly condemned. St. Ambrose pointed out to the Emperor that such a question as the orthodoxy of two persons could be settled by a local council in Italy; and as a result, by the Emperor's mandate, a council of Italian bishops met at Aquileia, other bishops having also permission to attend. Palladius and Secundianus were condemned, and these letters have reference to the proceedings at the council. They were probably written by St. Ambrose in the name of the council, A.D. 381.

13, 14. Two letters addressed to Theodosius, the former relating the decisions of a council, probably held at Milan, on the Meletian schism at Antioch, and the latter further expressing the desire of the bishops for a council on this subject, and also on the opinions of Apollinaris. Written A.D. 381 or 382.

15. To the Bishops of Macedonia, in reply to their notification of the death of Acholius, Bishop of Thessalonica, who baptized Theodosius, and had met St. Ambrose at a council in Rome. Written A.D. 383.

16. To Anicius, on his election to succeed Acholius, whose labours and life are commended by St. Ambrose. Written A.D. 383.

17, 18. On the occasion of the attempt of Symmachus and the heathen senators to procure the restitution of the image and Altar of Victory in the Roman Senate-house, frustrated by St. Ambrose, A.D. 384.

19. To Vigilius, Bishop of Trent, subsequently martyred, written probably about A.D. 385.

20. To his sister, Marcellina, giving an account of the frustrated attempts of the Arian and imperial party to gain possession of a basilica at Milan, A.D. 385,

21. To the Emperor Valentinian II., declining the challenge to dispute with the Arian Auxentius before lay judges. A.D. 386.

22. To his sister Marcellina, giving an account of the finding of the bodies of SS. Gervasius and Protasius, and of the consequent miracles. Written A.D. 386.

23. To the bishops of the province of Æmilia, on the proper date for the observance of Easter, in 387. Written A.D. 386.

24. To Valentinian II., with an account of St. Ambrose's second mission to Maximus on his behalf. Written probably A.D. 387.

25, 26. Inscribed the former to Studius, the second to Irenæus, but from internal evidence these appear to be the same person. It deals with the question, how far a judge being a Christian may lawfully sentence any one to death. Written probably about A.D. 388.

27–33. Addressed to Irenæus, on various questions. Written about A.D. 387.

34–36. To Orontianus, a cleric, on the soul and other questions. Written after 386.

37, 38. To Simplicianus, who became the successor of St. Ambrose in the see of Milan, setting forth that holiness is perfect freedom.

39. To Faustinus, on the occasion of the death of a sister. Written probably after A.D. 387.

40. To Theodosius. The Jewish synagogue at Callinicum in Mesopotamia having been destroyed by the Christians, and a meeting-house of the Valentinian heretics also burnt by the Catholics, Theodosius ordered that the bishop should rebuild the synagogue at his own expense, and the monks be punished. St. Ambrose remonstrates with the Emperor, and it would seem, from the following letter to his sister, at first unsuccessfully.

41. To his sister Marcellina, relating the circumstances alluded to above, and telling her of his sermon before the Emperor, and of his subsequent refusal to celebrate the Eucharist, until the Emperor had promised to rescind the order. The date of the two letters is A.D. 388.

42. Reply of St. Ambrose and a synod at Milan to the notification of Pope Siricius announcing the sentence of excommunication passed upon Jovinian and his followers. 43, 44. To Horontianus, in reply to his inquiries on some points connected with the Creation.

45. To Sabinus, Bishop of Placentia, in answer to questions concerning Paradise.

46. To the same, on the subject of an Apollinarian heretic.

47–49. To the same, with books and on private matters.

50. To Chromatius, probably Bishop of Aquileia, explaining how evil men may be used to utter true prophecies.

51. To Theodosius, after the massacre at Thessalonica. Written A.D. 390.

52. A private letter to Titianus.

53. To Theodosius, to express the sorrow of St. Ambrose at the death of Valentinian II., slain by Arbogastes.

54, 55. To Eusebius, not, it would seem, the Bishop of Bologna who was present at the Council of Aquileia, but rather a lay friend to whom St. Ambrose wrote his treatise on the training of a virgin. Probably written A.D. 392 or 393.

56. To Theophilus. The troubles of the church of Antioch through the Meletian schism might have terminated on the death of Paulinus, had he not on his deathbed consecrated Evagrius as his successor in violation of the canons. Theodosius, being pressed by the Western bishops, now summoned a council at Capua, commanding Flavian to attend, which command he however disobeyed. The council referred the matter to Theophilus of Alexandria

and the bishops of Egypt. But Flavian, as Theophilus had informed St. Ambrose, refused to submit to their decision. This is the reply of St. Ambrose advising Theophilus to summon Flavian once more, and communicate the result to Pope Siricius. The letter must have been written quite at the end of A.D. 391, or the beginning of 392.

57. To Eugenius the usurper, to avoid whom St. Ambrose had left Milan, and to whose letters he had sent no reply. Written A.D. 393.

58. To Sabinus, Bishop, on the resolution of Paulinus and Therasia to forsake the world. Written probably A.D. 393.

59. To Severus, Bishop probably of Naples, telling him of James, a Persian priest, who had resolved to retire from the world into Campania, and contrasting this with his own troubles, owing to the invasion of Eugenius, A.D. 393 or 394.

60. To Paternus, against a proposed incestuous marriage.

61. To Theodosius, after his victory over Eugenius. Written A.D. 394.

62. To the same, urging him to be merciful to the followers of Eugenius. Written in the same year.

63. To the Church at Vercellæ. The second division of the letters, being those which cannot be dated, begins here in the Benediction Edition.

64. To Irenæus, on the Manna.

65. To Simplicianus, on Exodus xxiv. 6.

66. To Romulus, on Aaron's making the calf of the golden earrings.

67. To Simplicianus, showing how Moses yielded to Aaron in matters relating to his priestly character.

68. To Romulus. Explanation of the text Deut. xxviii. 23.

69. To Irenæus, answering a question as to the prohibition under severe penalties in the Mosaic law, of disguising the sex by dress.

70, 71. To Horontianus, on part of the prophecy of Micah.

72. To Constantius, on the rite of circumcision.

73–76. To Irenæus. Why the law was given, and the scope of the Epistle to the Ephesians. The letter numbered 75 is plainly a continuation of 74, although inscribed to Clementianus, a difficulty similar to that about letter 26.

77, 78. To Horontianus, contrasting the condition of the Jew and the Christian.

79, 80. To Bellicius, on recovery from sickness, and on the miracle of healing the man blind from his birth.

81. To certain clergy, against despondency.

82. To Marcellus, concerning a lawsuit.

83. To Sisinnius, commending him for forgiving his son, who had married without consulting him.

84. To Cynegius.

85, 86. To Siricius, with thanks for letters, and commending Priscus.

87. To Segatius [more probably Phæbadius], Bishop of Agens, and Delphinus, Bishop of Bordeaux. Polybius, mentioned in the letter, was proconsul of Africa between the years 380 and 390.

88. To Atticus. Commendation of Priscus.

89. To Alypius. Acknowledgment of letters.

90. To Antonius. On the mutual affection of himself and St. Ambrose.

91. To Candidianus, probably a fellow-bishop. A letter of affection.

VI. HYMNS.

During the persecutions stirred up by the Arian Empress Justina, A.D. 385–6, referred to in his 20th letter, St. Ambrose and the faithful spent the whole night in the basilica, and the holy Bishop employed the people in singing psalms and hymns. A large number of hymns have been attributed to St. Ambrose, the number having by some editors been brought down to twelve, of which, however, only four are certainly his compositions.

1. *Eterne rerum Conditor,* referred to by St. Augustine, *Retract.* I. 21, and by St. Ambrose himself, *Hexaëm.* V. 24, 88. The hymn is still in use at Lauds on Sunday.

2. *Deus Creator omnium.* Quoted by St. Augustine, *Conf.* IX. 12, 32.

3. *Jam surigit hora tertia.* Also quoted by St. Augustine.

4. *Veni Redemptor gentium.* A Christmas hymn, quoted by Pope Celestine, A.D. 430, in a sermon against the Nestorians, preached before a synod at Rome, and also by other writers. Of other hymns one commencing, *Illuminans Altissimus,* is quoted by Cassiodorus as an Epiphany hymn by St. Ambrose, and the same author refers to another, *Orabo mente Dominum.* The Benedictine Editors admit six other hymns, but they are supported by no authority anterior to Venerable Bede.

VII. DOUBTFUL AND SPURIOUS WORKS.

This volume cannot of course comprehend the arguments and discussions necessary for any critical examination of certain works whether doubtful or certainly spurious, but their names may be given and certain conclusions stated.

1. Five books on the Jewish war, ordinarily attributed to Hegisippus. This is a translation into Latin and a condensation in part of the well-known work of Josephus. Ihm, a very thorough student of St. Ambrose, seems quite disposed to maintain after careful examination that this is the work of St. Ambrose.

2. *De lege Dei.* This treatise, a sort of compendium of Roman law in the fourth century, and comparison of it with the law of Moses, is ascribed, in a translation published by Mai, to St. Ambrose, who is said to have undertaken the work at the command of Theodosius. On the authenticity, however, of this treatise there probably will always remain much doubt.

3. Among works more or less doubtful are *De Sacramentis,* admitted by the Benedictines, but rejected, and apparently on sufficient grounds, by Ihm.

4. *Apologia David altera.* Suspected by Erasmus, Tillemont, and Ihm.

5. *De lapsu Virginis consecratæ.* A severe castigation of a fallen virgin and of her seducer. The treatise seems to have been written by a certain Bishop of Nicetas, and a MS. at speaks of it as having been revised by St. Ambrose.

6. There are further three brief addresses ascribed by some persons to St. Ambrose, touching on the question of selling all and giving to the poor. Some of the matter is like St. Ambrose, but the same cannot be said of the diction and style.

VIII. Lost Writings of St. Ambrose.

1. *Expositio Isaiæ prophetiæ*, referred to by St. Augustine as well as by St. Ambrose himself.

2. *Liber de Sacramento regenerationis sive de philosophia,* referred to by St. Augustine.

3. *Libellus ad Pansophium puerum,* written A.D. 393–4, according to Paulinus in his life of St. Ambrose.

4. *Libri quatuor regnorum,* referred to in the introduction to the work on the Jewish war.

5. *Expositio fidei,* quoted by Theodoret and others as a writing of St. Ambrose.

On Repentance.

Introduction

THESE two books were written against the Novatian heresy, which took its name, and to a considerable extent its form, from Novatus, a priest of the Church of Carthage, and Novatian, schismatically consecrated bishop at Rome. It was the outcome of a struggle which had long existed in the Church upon the question of the restitution to Church privileges of those who had fallen into grievous sin, and the possibility of their repentance.

The severest ground was taken by the Novatians, who were condemned successively by many councils, which maintained the power of the Church to admit those guilty of any sin whatsoever to repentance, and prescribed various rules and penalties applicable to different cases. The heresy, however, lasted for some time, becoming weaker in the fifth century, and gradually fading away as a separate body with a distinctive name. "Novatianism, in the tests which it used, its efforts after a perfectly pure communion, its crotchetty interpretations of Scripture, and many other features, presents a striking parallel to

many modern sects." [See *Dict. Chr. Biog.,* Blunt, Sects and heresies,
Ceillier, II. 427, etc.]

St. Ambrose, in writing against the Novatians, seems to have had some recent publication of theirs in his mind, which is now unknown. He begins by commending gentleness, a quality singularly wanting in the sect; speaks of the power committed to the Church of forgiving the greatest sins, and points out how God is more inclined to mercy than to severity, and refutes the arguments of the Novatians based on certain passages of Holy Scripture. In the second book, after urging the necessity of careful and speedy repentance, and the necessity of confessing one's sins, St. Ambrose meets the Novatian arguments based on Heb. vi. 4–6, from which they inferred the impossibility of restoration; and on St. Matt. xii. 31, 32, our Lord's words concerning sin against the Holy Spirit.

As regards the date of this treatise, it must have been somewhat before the exposition of Ps. xxxvii., which refers to it, but there is nothing else which can be taken as a certain guide. Possibly the Benedictine Editors are right in assigning it to about A.D. 384.
Some few persons, probably on doctrinal grounds, have been led to question the authorship of this treatise, but it is quoted by St. Augustine, and there has never been any real doubt on the subject.

ON REPENTANCE.

BOOK I.

CHAPTER I.

St. Ambrose writes in praise of gentleness, pointing out how needful that grace is for the rulers of the Church, and commended to them by the meekness of Christ. As the Novatians have fallen away from this, they cannot be considered disciples of Christ. Their pride and harshness are inveighed against.

1. IF the highest end of virtue is that which aims at the advancement of most, gentleness is the most lovely of all, which does not hurt even those whom it condemns, and usually renders those whom it condemns worthy of absolution. Moreover, it is the only virtue which has led to the increase of the Church which the Lord sought at the price of His own Blood, imitating the lovingkindness of heaven, and aiming at the redemption of all, seeks this end with a gentleness which the ears of men can endure, in presence of which their hearts do not sink, nor their spirits quail.

2. For he who endeavors to amend the faults of human weakness ought to bear this very weakness on his own shoulders, let it weigh upon himself, not cast it off. For we read that the Shepherd in the Gospel carried the weary sheep, and did not cast it off. And Solomon says: "Be not overmuch righteous;" for restraint should temper righteousness. For how shall he offer himself to you for healing whom you despise, who thinks that he will be an object of contempt, not of compassion, to his physician?

3. Therefore had the Lord Jesus compassion upon us in order to call us to Himself, not frighten us away. He came in meekness, He came in humility, and so He said: "Come unto Me, all ye that labor and are heavy laden, and I will refresh you." So, then, the Lord Jesus refreshes, and does not shut out nor cast off, and fitly chose such disciples as should be interpreters of the Lord's will, as should gather together and not drive away the people of God. Whence it is clear that they are not to be counted amongst the disciples of Christ, who think that harsh and proud opinions should be followed rather than such as are gentle and meek; persons who, while they themselves seek God's mercy, deny it to others, such as are the teachers of the Novatians, who call themselves pure.

4. What can show more pride than this, since the Scripture says: "No one is free from sin, not even an infant of a day old;" and David cries out: "Cleanse me from my sin." Are they more holy than David, of whose family Christ vouchsafed to be born in the mystery of the Incarnation, whose descendant is that heavenly Hall which received the world's Redeemer in her virgin womb? For what is more harsh than to inflict a penance which they do not relax, and by refusing pardon to take away the incentive to penance and repentance? Now no one can repent to good purpose unless he hopes for mercy.

CHAPTER II.

The assertion of the Novatians that they refuse communion only to the lapsed agrees neither with the teaching of holy Scripture nor with their own. And whereas they allege as a pretext their reverence for the divine power, they really are contemning it, inasmuch as it is a sign of low estimation not to use the whole of a power entrusted to one. But the Church rightly claims the power of binding and loosing, which heretics have not, inasmuch as she has received it from the Holy Spirit, against Whom they act presumptuously.

5. BUT they say that those should not be restored to communion who have fallen into denial of the faith. If they made the crime of sacrilege the only exception to receiving forgiveness, they would be acting harshly indeed, and, as it would seem, would be in opposition to the divine utterances only, while consistent with their own assertions. For when the Lord forgave all sins, He made an exception of none. But since, as it were after the fashion of the Stoics, they think that all sins are equal in gravity, and assert that he who has stolen a common fowl, as they say, no less than he who has smothered his father, should be forever excluded from the divine mysteries, how can they select those guilty of one special offence, since even they themselves cannot deny that it is most unjust that the penalty of one should extend to many?

6. They affirm that they are showing great reverence for God, to Whom alone they reserve the power of forgiving sins. But in truth none do Him greater injury than they who choose to prune His commandments and reject the office entrusted to them. For inasmuch as the Lord Jesus Himself said in the Gospel: "Receive ye the Holy Spirit: whosesoever sins ye forgive they are forgiven unto them, and whosesoever sins ye retain, they are retained," who is

it that honors Him most, he who obeys His bidding or he who rejects it?

7. The Church holds fast its obedience on either side, by both retaining and remitting sin; heresy is on the one side cruel, and on the other disobedient; wishes to bind what it will not loosen, and will not loosen what it has bound, whereby it condemns itself by its own sentence. For the Lord willed that the power of binding and of loosing should be alike, and sanctioned each by a similar condition. So he who has not the power to loose has not the power to bind. For as, according to the Lord's word, he who has the power to bind has also the power to loose, their teaching destroys itself, inasmuch as they who deny that they have the power of loosing ought also to deny that of binding. For how can the one be allowed and the other disallowed? It is plain and evident that either each is allowed or each is disallowed in the case of those to whom each has been given. Each is allowed to the Church, neither to heresy, for this power has been entrusted to priests alone. Rightly, therefore, does the Church claim it, which has true priests; heresy, which has not the priests of God, cannot claim it. And by not claiming this power heresy pronounces its own sentence, that not possessing priests it cannot claim priestly power. And so in their shameless obstinacy a shamefaced acknowledgment meets our view.

8. Consider, too, the point that he who has received the Holy Ghost has also received the power of forgiving and of retaining sin. For thus it is written: "Receive the Holy Spirit: whosesoever sins ye forgive, they are forgiven unto them, and whosesoever sins ye retain, they are

retained." So, then, he who has not received power to forgive sins has not received the Holy Spirit. The office of the priest is a gift of the Holy Spirit, and His right it is specially to forgive and to retain sins. How, then, can they claim His gift who distrust His power and His right?

9. And what is to be said of their excessive arrogance? For although the Spirit of God is more inclined to mercy than to severity, their will is opposed to that which He wills, and they do that which He wills not; whereas it is the office of a judge to punish, but of mercy to forgive. It would be more endurable, Novatian, that thou shouldst forgive than that thou shouldst bind. In the one case thou wouldst assume the right as one who rarely offended; in the other thou wouldst forgive as one who had fellow-feeling with the misery of sin.

CHAPTER III.

To the argument of the Novatians, that they only deny forgiveness in the case of greater sins, St. Ambrose replies, that this is also an offence against God, Who gave the power to forgive all sins, but that of course a more severe penance must follow in case of graver sins. He points out likewise that this distinction as to the gravity of sins assigns, as it were, severity to God, Whose mercy in the Incarnation is overlooked by the Novatians.

10. But they say that, with the exception of graver sins, they grant forgiveness to those of less weight. This is not the teaching of your father, Novatian, who thought that no one should be admitted to penance, considering that what he was unable to loose he would not bind, lest by binding he should inspire the hope that he would loose. So that your father is condemned by your own sentence, you who make a distinction between sins, some of which you consider that you can loose, and others which you consider to be without remedy. But God does not make a distinction, Who has promised His mercy to all, and granted to His priests the power of loosing without any exception. But he who has heaped up sin must also increase his penitence. For greater sins are washed away by greater weeping. So neither is Novatian justified, who excluded all from pardon; nor are you, who imitate and, at the same time, condemn him, for you diminish zeal for penance where it ought to be increased, since the mercy of Christ has taught us that graver sins must be made good by greater efforts.

11. And what perversity it is to claim for yourselves what can be forgiven, and, as you say, to reserve to God what cannot be forgiven. This would be to reserve to oneself the cases for mercy, to God those for severity. And what

as to that saying: "Let God be true but every man a liar, as it is written, That Thou mightest be justified in Thy words, and overcome when Thou art judged"? In order, then, that we may recognize that the God of mercy is rather prone to indulgence than to severity, it is said: "I desire mercy rather than sacrifice." How, then, can your sacrifice, who refuse mercy, be acceptable to God, since He says that He wills not the death of a sinner, but his correction?

12. Interpreting which truth, the Apostle says: "For God, sending His own Son in the likeness of sinful flesh, and for sin condemned sin in the flesh, that the righteousness of the Law might be fulfilled in us." He does not say "in the likeness of flesh," for Christ took on Himself the reality not the likeness of flesh; nor does He say in the likeness of sin, for He did no sin, but was made sin for us. Yet He came "in the likeness of sinful flesh;" that is, He took on Him the likeness of sinful flesh, the *likeness,* because it is written: "He is man, and who shall know Him?" He was man in the flesh, according to His human nature, that He might be recognized, but in power was above man, that He might not be recognized, so He has our flesh, but has not the failings of this flesh.

13. For He was not begotten, as is every man, by intercourse between male and female, but born of the Holy Spirit and of the Virgin; He received a stainless body, which not only no sins polluted, but which neither the generation nor the conception had been stained by any admixture of defilement. For we men are all born under sin, and our very origin is in evil, as we read in the words of David: "For lo, I was conceived in wickedness, and in sin did my mother bring me forth." Therefore the flesh of

Paul was a body of death, as he himself says: "Who shall deliver me from the body of this death?" But the flesh of Christ condemned sin, which He felt not at His birth, and crucified by His death, so that in our flesh there might be justification through grace, in which before there had been pollution by guilt.

14. What, then, shall we say to this, except that which the Apostle said: "If God is for us, who is against us? He who spared not His own Son, but gave Him up for us all, how has He not with Him also given us all things? Who shall lay a charge against the elect? It is God Who justifieth, who is he that shall condemn? It is Christ Who died, yea, Who also rose again, Who is at the right hand of God, Who also maketh intercession for us." Novatian then brings charges against those for whom Christ intercedes. Those whom Christ has redeemed unto salvation Novatian condemns to death. Those to whom Christ says: "Take My yoke upon you, and learn of Me, for I am gentle," Novatian says, I am not gentle. On those to whom Christ says: "Ye shall find rest for your souls, for My yoke is pleasant and My burden is light," Novatian lays a heavy burden and a hard yoke.

CHAPTER IV.

St. Ambrose proceeds with the proof of the divine mercy, and shows by the testimony of the Gospels that it prevails over severity, and he adduces the instance of athletes to show that of those who have denied Christ before men, all are not to be esteemed alike.

15. Although what has been said sufficiently shows how inclined the Lord Jesus is to mercy, let Him further instruct us with His own words, when He would arm us against the assaults of persecution. "Fear not," He says, "those who kill the body, but cannot kill the soul, but rather fear Him Who can cast both body and soul into hell." And farther on: "Every one, therefore, who shall confess Me before men, him will I also confess before My Father, Who is in heaven, but he who shall deny Me before men, him will I also deny before My Father, Who is in heaven."

16. Where He says that He will confess, He will confess "every one." Where He speaks of denying, He does not speak of denying "every one." For, whereas in the former clause He says, "Everyone who shall confess Me, him will I confess," we should expect that in the following clause He would also say, "Everyone who shall deny Me." But in order that He might not appear to deny every one, He concludes: "But he who shall deny Me before men, him will I also deny." He promises favor to everyone, but He does not threaten the penalty to everyone. He makes more of that which is merciful. He makes less of what is penal.

17. And this is written not only in that book of the Gospel of the Lord Jesus, which is written according to Matthew, but it is also to be read in that which we have according to

Luke, that we might know that neither had thus related the saying by chance.

18. We have said that it is thus written. Let us now consider the meaning. "Every one," He says, "who shall confess Me," that is to say, of whatever age, of whatever condition he may be, who shall confess Me, he shall have Me as the Rewarder of his confession. Whereas the expression is, "every one," no one who shall confess is excluded from the reward. But it is not said in like manner, "Everyone who shall deny shall be denied," for it is possible that a man overcome by torture may deny God in word, and yet worship Him in his heart.

19. Is the case the same with him who denies voluntarily, and with him whom torture, not his own will, has led to denial? How unfit were it, since with men credit is given for endurance in a struggle, that one should assert that it had no value with God! For often in this world's athletic contests the public crown together with the victors even the vanquished whose conduct has been approved, especially if perchance they have seen that they lost the victory by some trick or fraud. And shall Christ suffer His athletes, whom He has seen to yield for a moment to severe torments, to remain without forgiveness?

20. Shall not He take account of their toil, Who will not cast off for ever even those whom He casts off? For David says: "God will not cast off forever," and in opposition to this shall we listen to heresy asserting, "He does cast off forever"? David says: "God will not forever cut off His mercy from generation to generation, nor will He forget to be merciful." This is the prophet's

declaration, and there are those who would maintain a forgetfulness of mercy on God's part.

CHAPTER V.

The objection from the unchangeableness of God is answered from several passages of Scripture, wherein God promises forgiveness to sinners on their repentance. St. Ambrose also shows that mercy will be more readily accorded to such as have sinned, as it were, against their will, which he illustrates by the case of prisoners taken in war, and by language put into the mouth of the devil.

21. BUT they say that they make these assertions in order not to seem to make God liable to change, as He would be if He forgave those with whom He was angry. What then? Shall we reject the utterances of God and follow their opinions? But God is not to be judged by the statements of others, but by His own words. What mark of His mercy have we more ready at hand than that He Himself, through the prophet Hosea, is at once merciful as though reconciled to those whom in His anger He had threatened? For He says: "O Ephraim, what shall I do unto thee, or what shall I do unto thee, O Judah? Your kindness," etc. And further on: "How shall I establish thee? I will make thee as Admah, and as Zeboim." In the midst of His indignation He hesitates, as it were, with fatherly love, doubting how He can give over the wanderer to punishment; for although the Jew deserves it, God yet takes counsel with Himself. For immediately after having said, "I will make thee as Admah and as Zeboim," which cities, owing to their nearness to Sodom, suffered together in like destruction, He adds, "My heart is turned against Me, My compassion is aroused, I will not do according to the fierceness of Mine anger."

22. Is it not evident that the Lord Jesus is angry with us when we sin in order that He may convert us through fear of His indignation? His indignation, then, is not the

carrying out of vengeance, but rather the working out of forgiveness, for these are His words: "If thou shalt turn and lament, thou shalt be saved." He waits for our lamentations here, that is, in time, that He may spare us those which shall be eternal. He waits for our tears, that He may pour forth His goodness. So in the Gospel, having pity on the tears of the widow, He raised her son. He waits for our conversion, that He may Himself restore us to grace, which would have continued with us had no fall overtaken us. But He is angry because we have by our sins incurred guilt, in order that we may be humbled; we are humbled, in order that we may be found worthy rather of pity than of punishment.

23. Jeremiah, too, may certainly teach when he says: "For the Lord will not cast off for ever; for after He has humbled, He will have compassion according to the multitude of His mercies, Who hath not humbled from His whole heart nor cast off the children of men." This passage we certainly find in the Lamentations of Jeremiah, and from it, and from what follows, we note that the Lord humbles all the prisoners of the earth under His feet, in order that we may escape His judgment. But He does not bring down the sinner even to the earth with His whole heart Who raises the poor even from the dust and the needy from the dunghill. For He brings not down with His whole heart Who reserves the intention of forgiving.

24. But if He brings not down every sinner with His whole heart, how much less does He bring down him with His whole heart who has not sinned with his whole heart! For as He said of the Jews: "This people honoreth Me

with their lips, but their heart is far from Me," so perhaps He may say of some of the fallen: "They denied Me with their lips, but in heart they are with Me. It was pain which overcame them, not unfaithfulness which turned them aside." But some without cause refuse pardon to those whose faith the persecutor himself confessed up to the point of striving to overcome it by torture. They denied the Lord once, but confess Him daily; they denied Him in word, but confess Him with groans, with cries, and with tears; they confess Him with willing words, not under compulsion. They yielded, indeed, for a moment to the temptation of the devil, but even the devil afterwards departed from those whom he was unable to claim as his own. He yielded to their weeping, he yielded to their repentance, and after making them his own lost those whom he attached when they belonged to Another.

25. Is not the case such as when any one carries away captive the people of a conquered city? The captive is led away, but against his will. He must of necessity go to foreign lands, does not willingly make the journey; he takes his native land with him in his heart, and seeks an opportunity to return. What then? When any such return, does anyone urge that they should not be received; with less honor indeed, but with readier will, that the enemy may have nothing with which to reproach them? If you pardon an armed man who was able to fight, do you not pardon him in whom faith alone waged the battle?

26. If we were to enquire what is the opinion of the devil concerning those who have fallen after this sort, would he not probably reply: "This people honors me with their lips, but their heart is far from me? For how can he be

with me who does not depart from Christ? Without any cause do they appear to honor me who keep the doctrine of Jesus, and I thought that they would teach mine. They condemn me all the more when they forsake me after trial. Indeed Jesus is more glorified in these, when He receives them on their return to Him. All the angels rejoice, for in heaven there is greater joy over one sinner that repents, than over ninety and nine just persons who need not repentance. I am triumphed over in heaven and on earth. Christ loses nothing when they who came to me with weeping return with longing to the Church, and I am in danger even as regards my own, who will learn that in reality there is nothing here where men are led on by present rewards, but that there must be very much there where groans and tears and fasts are preferred to my feasts."

CHAPTER VI.

The Novatians, by excluding such from the banquet of Christ, imitate not indeed the good Samaritan, but the proud lawyer, the priest, and the Levite who are blamed in the Gospel, and are indeed worse than these.

27. Do you then, O Novatians, shut out these? For what is it when you refuse the hope of forgiveness but to shut out? But the Samaritan did not pass by the man who had been left half dead by the robbers; he dressed his wounds with oil and wine, first pouring in oil in order to comfort them; he set the wounded man on his own beast, on which he bore all his sins; nor did the Shepherd despise His wandering sheep.

28. But you say: "Touch me not." You who wish to justify yourselves say, "He is not our neighbor," being more proud than that lawyer who wished to tempt Christ, for he said "Who is my neighbor?" He asked, you deny, going on like that priest, like that Levite passing by him whom you ought to have taken and tended, and not receiving them into the inn for whom Christ paid the two pence, whose neighbor Christ bids you to become that you might show mercy to him. For he is our neighbor whom not only a similar condition has joined, but whom mercy has bound to us. You make yourself strange to him through pride, in vain puffing up yourself in your carnal mind, and not holding the Head. For if you held the Head you would consider that you must not forsake him for whom Christ died. If you held the Head you would consider that the whole body, by joining together rather than by separating, grows unto the increase of God[2948] by the bond of charity and the rescue of a sinner.

29. When, then, you take away all the fruits of repentance, what do you say but this: Let no one who is wounded enter our inn, let no one be healed in our Church? With us the sick are not cared for, we are whole, we have no need of a physician, for He Himself says: "They that are whole need not a physician, but they that are sick."

CHAPTER VII.

St. Ambrose, addressing Christ, complains of the Novatians, and shows that they have no part with Christ, Who wishes all men to be saved.

30. So, then, Lord Jesus, come wholly to Thy Church, since Novatian makes excuse. Novatian says, "I have bought a yoke of oxen," and he puts not on the light yoke of Christ, but lays upon his shoulders a heavy burden which he is not able to bear. Novatian held back Thy servants by whom he was invited, treated them contemptuously and slew them, polluting them with the stain of a reiterated baptism. Send forth, therefore, into the highways, and gather together good and bad, bring the weak, the blind, and the lame into Thy Church. Command that Thy house be filled, bring in all unto Thy supper, for Thou wilt make him whom Thou shalt call worthy, if he follow Thee. He indeed is rejected who has not the wedding garment, that is, the vestment of charity, the veil of grace. Send forth I pray Thee to all.

31. Thy Church does not excuse herself from Thy supper, Novatian makes excuse. Thy family says not, "I am whole, I need not the physician," but it says: "Heal me, O Lord, and I shall be healed; save me, and I shall be saved." The likeness of Thy Church is that woman who went behind and touched the hem of Thy garment, saying within herself: "If I do but touch His garment I shall be whole." So the Church confesses her wounds, but desires to be healed.

32. And Thou indeed, O Lord, desirest that all should be healed, but all do not wish to be healed. Novatian wishes

not, who thinks that he is whole. Thou, O Lord, sayest that Thou art sick, and feelest our infirmity in the least of us, saying: "I was sick and ye visited Me." Novatian does not visit that least one in whom Thou desirest to be visited. Thou saidst to Peter when he excused himself from having his feet washed by Thee: "If I wash not thy feet, thou wilt have no part with Me." What fellowship, then, can they have with Thee, who receive not the keys of the kingdom of heaven, saying that they ought not to remit sins?

33. And this confession is indeed rightly made by them, for they have not the succession of Peter, who hold not the chair of Peter, which they rend by wicked schism; and this, too, they do, wickedly denying that sins can be forgiven even in the Church, whereas it was said to Peter: "I will give unto thee the keys of the kingdom of heaven, and whatsoever thou shalt bind on earth shall be bound also in heaven, and whatsoever thou shalt loose on earth shall be loosed also in heaven." And the vessel of divine election himself said: "If ye have forgiven anything to anyone, I forgive also, for what I have forgiven I have done it for your sakes in the person of Christ." Why, then, do they read Paul's writings, if they think that he has erred so wickedly as to claim for himself the right of his Lord? But he claimed what he had received, he did not usurp that which was not due to him.

CHAPTER VIII.

It was the Lord's will to confer great gifts on His disciples. Further, the Novatians confute themselves by the practices of laying on of hands and of baptism, since it is by the same power that sins are remitted in penance and in baptism. Their conduct is then contrasted with that of our Lord.

34. It is the will of the Lord that His disciples should possess great powers; it is His will that the same things which He did when on earth should be done in His Name by His servants. For He said: "Ye shall do greater things than these." He gave them power to raise the dead. And whereas He could Himself have restored to Saul the use of his sight, He nevertheless sent him to His disciple Ananias, that by his blessing Saul's eyes might be restored, the sight of which he had lost. Peter also He bade walk with Himself on the sea, and because he faltered He blamed him for lessening the grace given him by the weakness of his faith. He Who Himself was the light of the world granted to His disciples to be the light of the world through grace. And because He purposed to descend from heaven and to ascend thither again, He took up Elijah into heaven to restore him again to earth at the time which should please Him. And being baptized with the Holy Spirit and with fire, He foreshadowed the Sacrament of Baptism at the hands of John.

35. And in fine He gave all gifts to His disciples, of whom He said: "In My Name they shalt cast out devils; they shall speak with new tongues; they shall take up serpents; and if they shall drink any deadly thing it shall not hurt them; they shall lay hands on the sick, and they shall do

well." So, then, He gave them all things, but there is no power of man exercised in these things, in which the grace of the divine gift operates.

36. Why, then, do you lay on hands, and believe it to be the effect of the blessing, if perchance some sick person recovers? Why do you assume that any can be cleansed by you from the pollution of the devil? Why do you baptize if sins cannot be remitted by man? If baptism is certainly the remission of all sins, what difference does it make whether priests claim that this power is given to them in penance or at the font? In each the mystery is one.

37. But you say that the grace of the mysteries works in the font. What works, then, in penance? Does not the Name of God do the work? What then? Do you, when you choose, claim for yourselves the grace of God, and when you choose reject it? But this is a mark of insolent presumption, not of holy fear, when those who wish to do penance are despised by you. You cannot, forsooth, endure the tears of the weepers; your eyes cannot bear the coarse clothing, the filth of the squalid; with proud eyes and puffed-up hearts you delicate ones say with angry tones, "Touch me not, for I am pure."

38. The Lord said indeed to Mary Magdalene, "Touch Me not," but He Who was pure did not say, "because I am pure." Do you, Novatian, dare to call yourself pure, whilst, even if you were pure as regards your acts, you would be made impure by this saying alone? Isaiah says: "O wretched that I am, and pricked to the heart; for that being a man, and having unclean lips, I dwell also in the midst of a people having unclean lips," and do you say, "I

am clean," when, as it is written, not even an infant of a
day old is pure? David says, "And cleanse me from my
sin," whom for his tender heart the grace of God often
cleansed; are you pure who are so unrighteous as to have
no tenderness, as to see the mote in your brother's eye,
but not to consider the beam which is in your own eye?
For with God no one who is unjust is pure. And what is
more unjust than to desire to have your sins forgiven you,
and yet yourself to think that he who entreats you ought
not to be forgiven? What is more unjust than to justify
yourself in that wherein you condemn another, whilst
you yourself are committing worse offences?

39. Then, too, the Lord Jesus when about to consecrate[2966]
the forgiveness of our sins replied to John, who said: "I
ought to be baptized of Thee, and comest Thou to me?
Suffer it now, for thus it becometh us to fulfill all
righteousness." And the Lord indeed came to a sinner,
though indeed He had no sin, and desired to be baptized,
having no need of cleansing; who, then, can tolerate you,
who think there is no need for you to be cleansed by
penance, because you say you are cleansed by grace, as
though it were now impossible for you to sin?

CHAPTER IX.

By collating similar passages with 1 Sam. iii. 25, St. Ambrose shows that the meaning is not that no one shall intercede, but that the intercessor must be worthy as were Moses and Jeremiah, at whose prayers we read that God spared Israel.

40. BUT you say, It is written: "If a man sin against the Lord, who shall entreat for him?" First of all, as I already said before, I might allow you to make that objection if you refused penance to those only who denied the faith. But what difficulty does that question produce? For it is not written, "No one shall entreat for him;" but, "Who shall entreat?" that is to say, the question is, Who in such a case can entreat? The entreaty is not excluded.

41. Then you have in the fifteenth Psalm: "Lord, who shall dwell in Thy tabernacle, or who shall rest upon Thy holy hill?" It is not that no one, but that he who is approved shall dwell there, nor does it say that no one shall rest, but he who is chosen shall rest. And that you may know that this is true, it is said not much later in the twenty-fourth Psalm: "Who shall ascend into the hill of the Lord, or who shall stand in His holy place?" The writer implies, not any ordinary person, or one of the common sort, but only a man of excellent life and of singular merit. And that we may understand that when the question is asked, Who? it does not imply no one, but some special one is meant, after having said "Who shall ascend into the hill of the Lord?" the Psalmist adds: "He that hath clean hands and a pure heart, who hath not lift up his mind unto vanity." And elsewhere it is said: "Who is wise and he shall understand these things?" And in the Gospel: "Who is the faithful and wise steward, whom the

Lord shall set over His household to give them their measure of wheat in due season?" And that we may understand that He speaks of such as really exist, the Lord added: "Blessed is that servant, whom his Lord when He cometh shall find so doing." And I am of opinion that where it is said, "Lord, who is like unto Thee?" it is not meant that none is like, for the Son is the image of the Father.

42. We must then understand in the same manner, "Who shall entreat for him?" as implying: It must be some one of excellent life who shall entreat for him who has sinned against the Lord. The greater the sin, the more worthy must be the prayers that are sought. For it was not any one of the common people who prayed for the Jewish people, but Moses, when forgetful of their covenant they worshipped the head of the calf. Was Moses wrong? Certainly he was not wrong in praying, who both merited and obtained that for which he asked. For what should such love not obtain as that of his when he offered himself for the people and said: "And now, if Thou wilt forgive their sin, forgive; but if not, blot me out of the book of life." We see that he does not think of himself, like a man full of fancies and scruples, whether he may incur the risk of some offence, as Novatian says he dreads that he might, but rather, thinking of all and forgetful of himself, he was not afraid lest he should offend, so that he might rescue and free the people from danger of offence.

43. Rightly, then, is it said: "Who shall entreat for him?" It implies that it must be such an one as Moses to offer himself for those who sin, or such as Jeremiah, who, though the Lord said to him, "Pray not thou for this

people," and yet he prayed and obtained their forgiveness. For at the intercession of the prophet, and the entreaty of so great a seer, the Lord was moved and said to Jerusalem, which had meanwhile repented for its sins, and had said: "O Almighty Lord God of Israel, the soul in anguish, and the troubled spirit crieth unto Thee, hear, O Lord, and have mercy." And the Lord bids them lay aside the garments of mourning, and to cease the groanings of repentance, saying: "Put off, O Jerusalem, the garment of thy mourning and affliction. And clothe thyself in beauty, the glory which God hath given thee forever."

CHAPTER X.

St. John did not absolutely forbid that prayer should be made for those who "sin unto death," since he knew that Moses, Jeremiah, and Stephen had so prayed, and he himself implies that forgiveness is not to be denied them.

44. Such intercessors, then, must be sought for after very grievous sins, for if any ordinary persons pray they are not heard.

45. So that point of yours will have no weight, which you take from the Epistle of John, where he says: "He who knows that his brother sinneth a sin not unto death, let him ask, and God will give him life, because he sinned not unto death. There is a sin unto death: not concerning it do I say, let him ask." He was not speaking to Moses and Jeremiah, but to the people, who must seek another intercessor for their sins; the people, for whom it is sufficient they entreat God for their lighter faults, and consider that pardon for weightier sins must be reserved for the prayers of the just. For how could John say that graver sins should not be prayed for, when he had read that Moses prayed and obtained his request, where there had been willful casting off of faith, and knew that Jeremiah also had entreated?

46. How could John say that we should not pray for the sin unto death, who himself in the Apocalypse wrote the message to the angel of the Church of Pergamos? "Thou hast there those that hold the doctrine of Balaam, who taught Balac to put a stumbling-block before the children of Israel, to eat things sacrificed unto idols, and to commit fornication. So hast thou also them that hold the doctrines of the Nicolaitans. Repent likewise, or else I will come to

thee quickly." Do you see that the same God Who requires repentance promises forgiveness? And then He says: "He that hath ears let him hear what the Spirit saith to the churches: To him that overcometh will I give to eat of the hidden manna."

47. Did not John himself know that Stephen prayed for his persecutors, who had not been able even to listen to the Name of Christ, when he said of those very men by whom he was being stoned: "Lord, lay not this sin to their charge"? And we see the result of this prayer in the case of the Apostle, for Paul, who kept the garments of those who were stoning Stephen, not long after became an apostle by the grace of God, having before been a persecutor.

CHAPTER XI.

The passage quoted from St. John's Epistle is confirmed by another in which salvation is promised to those who believe in Christ, which refutes the Novatians who try to induce the lapsed to believe, although denying them pardon. Furthermore, many who had lapsed have received the grace of martyrdom, whilst the example of the good Samaritan shows that we must not abandon those in whom even the faintest amount of faith is still alive.

48. SINCE, then, we have spoken of the general Epistle of St. John, let us enquire whether the writings of John in the Gospel agree with your interpretation. For he writes that the Lord said: "God so loved this world, that He gave His only-begotten Son, that every one that believeth on Him should not perish but have everlasting life." If, then, you wish to reclaim any one of the lapsed, do you exhort him to believe, or not to believe? Undoubtedly you exhort him to believe. But, according to the Lord's words, he who believes shall have everlasting life. How, then, will you forbid to pray for him, who has a claim to everlasting life? since faith is of divine grace, as the Apostle teaches where he speaks of the differences of gifts, for "to another is given faith by the same Spirit." And the disciples say to the Lord: "Increase our faith." He then who has faith has life, and he who has life is certainly not shut out from pardon; "that everyone," it is said, "that believeth on Him should not perish." Since it is said, Everyone, no one is shut out, no one is excepted, for He does not except him who has lapsed, if only afterwards he believes effectually.

49. We find that many have at length recovered themselves after a fall, and have suffered for the Name of God. Can we deny fellowship with the martyrs to these to whom the Lord Jesus has not denied it? Do we dare to say

that life is not restored to those to whom Christ has given a crown? As, then, a crown is given to many after they have lapsed, so, too, if they believe, their faith is restored, which faith is the gift of God, as you read: "Because unto you it hath been granted by God not only to believe in Him, but also to suffer in His behalf."[2988] Is it possible that he who has the gift of God should not have His forgiveness?

50. Now it is not a single but a twofold grace that everyone who believes should also suffer for the Lord Jesus. He, then, who believes receives his grace, but he receives a second, if his faith be crowned by suffering. For neither was Peter without grace before he suffered, but when he suffered he received a second gift. And many who have not had the grace to suffer for Christ have nevertheless had the grace of believing on Him.

51. Therefore it is said: "That every one that believeth in Him should not perish." Let no one, that is, of whatever condition, after whatever fall, fear that he will perish. For it may come to pass that the good Samaritan of the Gospel may find someone going down from Jerusalem to Jericho, that is, falling back from the martyr's conflict to the pleasures of this life and the comforts of the world; wounded by robbers, that is, by persecutors, and left half dead; that good Samaritan, Who is the Guardian of our souls (for the word Samaritan means Guardian), may, I say, not pass by him but tend and heal him.

52. Perchance He therefore passes him not by, because He sees in him some signs of life, so that there is hope that he may recover. Does it not seem to you that he who has fallen is half alive if faith sustains any breath of life? For

he is dead who wholly casts God out of his heart. He, then, who does not wholly cast Him out, but under pressure of torments has denied Him for a time, is half dead. Or if he be dead, why do you bid him repent, seeing he cannot now be healed? If he be half dead, pour in oil and wine, not wine without oil, that may be the comfort and the smart. Place him upon thy beast, give him over to the host, lay out two pence for his cure, be to him a neighbor. But you cannot be a neighbor unless you have compassion on him; for no one can be called a neighbor unless he have healed, not killed, another. But if you wish to be called a neighbor, Christ says to you: "Go and do likewise."

CHAPTER XII.

Another passage of St. John is considered. The necessity of keeping the commandments of God may be complied with by those who, having fallen, repent, as well as by those who have not fallen, as is shown in the case of David.

53. LET us consider another similar passage: "He that believeth on the Son hath eternal life, but he that believeth not the Son shall not see life, but the wrath of God abideth on him." That which abideth has certainly had a commencement, and that from some offence, viz., that first he not believe. When, then, any one believes, the wrath of God departs and life comes. To believe, then, in Christ is to gain life, for "he that believeth in Him is not judged."

54. But with reference to this passage they allege that he who believes in Christ ought to keep His sayings, and say that it is written in the Lord's own words: "I am come a light into this world, that whosoever believeth in Me may not abide in darkness. And if any man hear My word and keep it, I judge him not." He judges not, and do you judge? He says, "that whosoever believeth on Me may not abide in darkness," that is, that if he be in darkness he may not remain therein, but may amend his error, correct his fault, and keep My commandments, for I have said, "I will not the death of the wicked, but the correction." I said above that he that believeth on Me is not judged, and I keep to this: "For I am not come to judge the world, but that the world may be saved through Me." I pardon willingly, I quickly forgive, "I will have mercy rather than sacrifice," because by sacrifice the just is rendered more acceptable, by mercy the sinner is redeemed. "I come not to call the righteous but sinners." Sacrifice was under the

Law, in the Gospel is mercy. "The Law was given by Moses, grace by Me."

55. And again further on He says: "He that despiseth Me, and receiveth not My words, hath one that judgeth him." Does he seem to you to have received Christ's words who has not corrected himself? Undoubtedly not. He, then, who corrects himself receives His word, for this is His word, that everyone should turn back from sin. So, then, of necessity you must either reject this saying of His, or if you cannot deny it you must accept it.

56. It is also necessary that he who leaves off sinning must keep the commandments of God and renounce his sins. We ought not, then, to interpret this saying of him who has always kept the commandments, for if this had been His meaning He would have added the word *always*, but by not adding it He shows that He was speaking of him who has kept what he has heard, and what he heard has led him to correct his faults; he has then kept what he has heard.

57. But how hard it is to condemn to penance for life one who even afterwards keeps the commandments of the Lord, let Him teach us Himself Who has not refused forgiveness. Even to those who do not keep His commandments, as you read in the Psalm: "If they profane My statutes and keep not My commandments, I will visit their offences with the rod and their sins with scourges, but My mercy will I not take from them." So, then, He promises mercy to all.

58. Yet that we may not think that this mercy is without judgment, there is a distinction made between those who have paid continual obedience to God's commandments, and those who at some time, either by error or by compulsion, have fallen. And that you may not think that it is only our arguments which press you, consider the decision of Christ, Who said: "If the servant knew his Lord's will and did it not, he shall be beaten with many stripes, but if he knew it not, he shall be beaten with few stripes." Each, then, if he believes, is received, for God "chasteneth every son whom He receiveth," and him whom He chasteneth He does not give over unto death, for it is written: "The Lord hath chastened me sore, but He hath not given me over unto death."

CHAPTER XIII.

They who have committed a "sin unto death" are not to be abandoned, but subjected to penance, according to St. Paul. Explanation of the phrase "Deliver unto Satan." Satan can afflict the body, but these afflictions bring spiritual profit, showing the power of God, Who thus turns Satan's devices against himself.

59. LASTLY, Paul teaches us that we must not abandon those who have committed a sin unto death, but that we must rather coerce them with the bread of tears and tears to drink, yet so that their sorrow itself be moderated. For this is the meaning of the passage: "Thou hast given them to drink in large measure," that their sorrow itself should have its measure, lest perchance he who is doing penance should be consumed by overmuch sorrow, as was said to the Corinthians: "What will ye? Shall I come to you with a rod, or in love and a spirit of meekness?" But even the rod is not severe, since he had read: "Thou shalt beat him indeed with the rod, but shalt deliver his soul from death."

60. What the Apostle means by the rod is shown by his invective against fornication, his denunciation of incest, his reprehension of pride, because they were puffed up who ought rather to be mourning, and lastly, his sentence on the guilty person, that he should be excluded from communion, and delivered to the adversary, not for the destruction of the soul but of the flesh. For as the Lord did not give power to Satan over the soul of holy Job, but allowed him to afflict his body, so here, too, the sinner is delivered to Satan for the destruction of the flesh, that the serpent might lick the dust3010 of his flesh, but not hurt his soul.

61. Let, then, our flesh die to lusts, let it be captive, let it be subdued, and not war against the law of our mind, but die in subjection to a good service, as in Paul, who buffeted his body that he might bring it into subjection, in order that his preaching might become more approved, if the law of his flesh agreed and was consonant with the law of his flesh. For the flesh dies when its wisdom passes over into the spirit, so that it no longer has a taste for the things of the flesh, but for the things of the spirit. Would that I might see my flesh growing weak, would that I were not dragged captive into the law of sin, would that I lived not in the flesh, but in the faith of Christ! And so there is greater grace in the infirmity of the body than in its soundness.

62. Having explained Paul's meaning, let us now consider the words themselves, in what sense he said that he had delivered him to Satan for the destruction of the flesh, for the devil it is who tries us. For he brings ailments on each of our limbs, and sickness on our whole bodies. And then, too, he smote holy Job with evil sores from the feet to the head, because he had received the power of destroying his flesh, when God said: "Behold, I give him up unto thee, only preserve his life." This the Apostle took up in the same words, giving up this man to Satan for the destruction of the flesh, that his spirit might be saved in the day of our Lord Jesus Christ.

63. Great is the power, great is the gift, which commands the devil to destroy himself. For he destroys himself when he makes the man whom he is seeking to overthrow by temptation stronger instead of weak, because whilst he is weakening the body he is strengthening his soul. For

sickness of the body restrains sin, but luxury sets on fire the sin of the flesh.

64. The devil is then deceived so as to wound himself with his own bite, and to arm against himself him whom he thought to weaken. So he armed holy Job the more after he wounded him, who, with his whole body covered with sores, endured indeed the bite of the devil, but felt not his poison. And so it is well said of him, "Thou shalt draw out the dragon with an hook, thou wilt play with him as with a bird, thou shalt bind him as a boy doth a sparrow, thou shalt lay thine hand upon him."

65. You see how he is mocked by Paul, so that, like the child in prophecy, he lays his hand on the hole of the asp, and the serpent injures him not; he draws him out of his hiding-places, and makes of his venom a spiritual antidote, so that what is venom becomes a medicine, the venom serves to the destruction of the flesh, it becomes medicine to the healing of the spirit. For that which hurts the body benefits the spirit.

66. Let, then, the serpent bite the earthy part of me, let him drive his tooth into my flesh, and bruise my body; and may the Lord say of me: "I give him up unto thee, only preserve his life." How great is the power of Christ, that the guardianship of man is made a charge even to the devil himself, who always desires to injure him. Let us then make the Lord Jesus favorable to ourselves. At the command of Christ the devil himself becomes the guardian of his prey. Even unwillingly he carries out the commands of heaven, and, though cruel, obeys the commands of gentleness.

67. But why do I commend his obedience? Let him be ever evil that God may be ever good, Who converts his ill-will into grace for us. He wishes to injure us, but cannot if Christ resist him. He wounds the flesh but preserves the life. And then it is written: "Then shall the wolves and the lambs feed together, the lion and the ox shall eat straw, and they shall not hurt nor destroy in My holy mountain, saith the Lord." For this is the sentence of condemnation on the serpent: "Dust shall be thy food." What dust? Surely that of which it is said: "Dust thou art, and into dust shalt thou return."

CHAPTER XIV.

*St. Ambrose explains that the flesh given to Satan for destruction is
eaten by the serpent when the soul is set free from carnal desires. He
gives, therefore, various rules for guarding the senses, points out the
snares laid for us by means of pleasures, and exhorts his hearers not
to fear the destruction of the flesh by the serpent.*

68. THE serpent eats this dust, if the Lord Jesus is
favorable to us, that our spirit may not sympathize with
the weakness of the flesh, nor be set on fire by the vapors
of the flesh and the heat of our members. "It is better to
marry than to burn," for there is a flame which burns
within. Let us not then suffer this fire to approach the
bosom of our minds and the depths of our hearts, lest we
burn up the covering of our inmost hearts, and lest the
devouring fire of lust consume this outward garment of
the soul and its fleshy veil, but let us pass through the fire.
And should any one fall into the fire of love let him leap
over it and pass forth; let him not bind to himself
adulterous lust with the bands of thoughts, let him not tie
knots around himself by the fastenings of continual
reflection, let him not too often turn his attention to the
form of a harlot, and let not a maiden lift her eyes to the
countenance of a youth. And if by chance she has looked
and is caught, how much more will she be entangled if
she gazes with curiosity.

69. Let custom itself teach us. A woman covers her face
with a veil for this reason, that in public her modesty may
be safe. That her face may not easily meet the gaze of a
youth, let her be covered with the nuptial veil, so that not
even in chance meetings she might be exposed to the
wounding of another or of herself, though the wound of
either were indeed hers. But if she cover her head with a

veil that she may not accidentally see or be seen (for when the head is veiled the face is hidden), how much more ought she to cover herself with the veil of modesty, so as even in public to have her own secret place.

70. But granted that the eye has fallen upon another, at least let not the inward affection follow. For to have seen is no sin, but one must be careful that it be not the source of sin. The bodily eye sees, but let the eye of the heart be closed; let modesty of mind remain. We have a Lord Who is both strict and indulgent. The prophet indeed said: "Look not upon the beauty of a woman that is all harlot." But the Lord said: "Whoever shall look on a woman to lust after her, hath committed adultery with her already in his heart." He does not say, "Whosoever shall look hath committed adultery," but "Whosoever shall look on her to lust after her." He condemned not the look but sought out the inward affection. But that modesty is praiseworthy which has so accustomed itself to close the bodily eyes as often not to see what we really behold. For we seem to behold with the bodily sight whatever meets us; but if there be not joined to this any attention of the mind, the sight also, according to what is usual in the body, fades away, so that in reality we see rather with the mind than with the body.

71. And if the flesh has seen the flame, let us not cherish that flame in our bosoms, that is, in the depths of the heart and the inward part of the mind. Let us not instill this fire into our bones, let us not bind bonds upon ourselves, let us not join in conversation with such as may be the cause to us of unholy fires. The speech of a maiden is a snare to a youth, the words of a youth are the bonds of love.

72. Joseph saw the fire when the woman eager for adultery spoke to him. She wished to catch him with her words. She set the snares of her lips, but was not able to capture the chaste man. For the voice of modesty, the voice of gravity, the rein of caution, the care for integrity, the discipline of chastity, loosed the woman's chains. So that unchaste person could not entangle him in her meshes. She laid her hand upon him; she caught his garment, that she might tighten the noose around him. The words of a lascivious woman are the snares of lust, and her hands the bonds of love; but the chaste mind could not be taken either by snares or by bonds. The garment was cast off, the bonds were loosed, and because he did not admit the fire into the bosom of his mind, his body was not burnt.

73. You see, then, that our mind is the cause of our guilt. And so the flesh is innocent, but is often the minister of sin. Let not, then, desire of beauty overcome you. Many nets and many snares are spread by the devil. The look of a harlot is the snare of him who loves her. Our own eyes are nets to us, wherefore it is written: "Be not taken with thine eyes." So, then, we spread nets for ourselves in which we are entangled and hampered. We bind chains on ourselves, as we read: "For everyone is bound with the chains of his own sins."

74. Let us then pass through the fires of youth and the glow of early years; let us pass through the waters, let us not remain therein, lest the deep floods shut us in. Let us rather pass over, that we too may say: "Our soul has passed over the stream," for he who has passed over is

safe. And lastly, the Lord speaks thus: "If thou pass through the water, I am with thee, the rivers shall not overflow thee." And the prophet says: "I have seen the wicked exalted above the cedars of Libanus, and I passed by, and lo, he was not." Pass by things of this world, and you will see that the high places of the wicked have fallen. Moses, too, passing by things of this world, saw a great sight and said: "I will turn aside and see this great sight," for had he been held by the fleeting pleasures of this world he would not have seen so great a mystery.

75. Let us also pass over this fire of lust, fearing which Paul—but fearing for us, inasmuch as by buffeting his body he had come no longer to fear for himself—says to us: "Flee fornication." Let us then flee it as though following us, though indeed it follows not behind us, but within our very selves. Let us then diligently take heed lest while we are fleeing from it we carry it with ourselves. For we wish for the most part to flee, but if we do not wholly cast it out of our mind, we rather take it up than forsake it. Let us then spring over it, lest it be said to us: "Walk ye in the flame of your fire, which ye have kindled for yourselves." For as he who "takes fire into his bosom burns his clothes," so he who walks upon fiery coals must of necessity burn his feet, as it is written: "Can one walk upon coals of fire and not burn his feet?"

76. This fire is dangerous, let us then not feed it with the fuel of luxury. Lust is fed by feastings, nourished by delicacies, kindled by wine, and inflamed by drunkenness. Still more dangerous than these are the incentives of words, which intoxicate the mind as it were with a kind of wine of the vine of Sodom. Let us be on our guard against

abundance of this wine, for when the flesh is intoxicated the mind totters, the heart wavers, the heart is carried to and fro. And so with regard to each that precept is useful wherein Timothy is warned: "Drink a little wine because of thy frequent infirmities." When the body is heated, it excites the glow of the mind; when the flesh is chilled with the cold of disease the spirit is chilled; when the body is in pain, the mind is sad, but the sadness shall become joy.

77. Do not then fear if your flesh be eaten away, the soul is not consumed. And so David says that he does not fear, because the enemy were eating up his flesh but not his soul, as we read: "When evil-doers come near upon me to eat up my flesh, my foes who trouble me, they were weakened and fell." So the serpent works overthrow for himself alone, therefore is he who has been injured by the serpent given over to the serpent that he may raise up again him whom he cast down, and the overthrow of the serpent may be the raising again of the man. And Scripture testifies that Satan is the author of this bodily suffering and weakness of the flesh, where Paul says: "There was given unto me a thorn in the flesh, a messenger of Satan to buffet me, that I should not be exalted." So Paul learned to heal even as he himself had been made whole.

CHAPTER XV.

Returning from this digression, St. Ambrose explains what is the meaning of St. Paul where he speaks of coming "with a rod or in the spirit of meekness." One who has grievously fallen is to be separated, but to be again restored to religious privileges when he has sufficiently repented. The old leaven is purged out when the hardness of the letter is tempered by the meal of a milder interpretation. All should be sprinkled with the Church's meal and fed with the food of charity, lest they become like that envious elder brother, whose example is followed by the Novatians.

78. THAT faithful teacher, having promised one of two things, gave each. He came with a rod, for he separated the guilty man from the holy fellowship. And well is he said to be delivered to Satan who is separated from the body of Christ. But he came in love and with the spirit of meekness, whether because he so delivered him up as to save his soul, or because he afterwards restored to the sacraments him whom he had before separated.

79. For it is needful to separate one who has grievously fallen, lest a little leaven corrupt the whole lump. And the old leaven must be purged out, or the old man in each person; that is, the outward man and his deeds, he who among the people has grown old in sin and hardened in vices. And well did he say purged, not cast forth, for what is purged is not considered wholly valueless, for to this end is it purged, that what is of value be separated from the worthless, but that which is cast forth is considered to have in itself nothing of value.

80. The Apostle then judged that the sinner should then at once be restored to the heavenly sacraments if he himself wished to be cleansed. And well is it said "Purge," for he

is purged as by certain things done by the whole people, and is washed in the tears of the multitude, and redeemed from sin by the weeping of the multitude, and is purged in the inner man. For Christ granted to His Church that one should be redeemed by means of all, as she herself was found worthy of the coming of the Lord Jesus, in order that through One all might be redeemed.

81. This is Paul's meaning which the words make more obscure. Let us consider the exact words of the Apostle: "Purge out," says he, "the old leaven, that ye may be a new lump, even as ye are unleavened." Either that the whole Church takes up the burden of the sinner, with whom she has to suffer in weeping and prayer and pain, and, as it were, covers herself with his leaven, in order that by means of all that which is to be done away in the individual doing penance may be purged by a kind of contribution and commixture of compassion and mercy offered with manly vigor. Or one may understand it as that woman in the Gospel teaches us, who is a type of the Church, when she hid the leaven in her meal, till all was leavened, and the whole could be used as pure.

82. The Lord taught me in the Gospel what leaven is when He said: "Do ye not understand that I said not concerning bread, Beware of the leaven of the Pharisees and Sadducees?" Then, it is said, they understood that He spake not of bread, but that they should beware of the doctrine of the Pharisees and Sadducees. This leaven, then—that is, the doctrine of the Pharisees and the contentiousness of the Sadducees—the Church hides in her meal, when she softened the hard letter of the Law by a spiritual interpretation, and ground it as it were in the

mill of her explanations, bringing out as it were from the husks of the letter the inner secrets of the mysteries, and setting forth the belief in the Resurrection, wherein the mercy of God is proclaimed, and wherein it is believed that the life of those who are dead is restored.

83. Now this comparison seems to be not unfitly brought forward in this place, since the kingdom of heaven is redemption from sin, and therefore we all, both bad and good, are mingled with the meal of the Church that we all may be a new lump. But that no one may be afraid that an admixture of evil leaven might injure the lump, the Apostle said: "That ye may be a new lump, even as ye are unleavened;" that is to say, This mixture will render you again such, as in the pure integrity of your innocence. If we thus have compassion, we are not stained with the sins of others, but we gain the restoration of another to the increase of our own grace, so that our integrity remains as it was. And therefore he adds: "For Christ our Passover is sacrificed for us;" that is, the Passion of the Lord profited all, and gave redemption to sinners who repented of the sins they had committed.

84. Let us then keep the feast on good food, doing penance yet joyful in our redemption, for no food is sweeter than kindness and gentleness. Let no envy towards the sinner who is saved be mingled with our feasts and joy, lest that envious brother, as is set forth in the Gospel, exclude himself from the house of his Father, because he grieved at the reception of his brother, at whose lasting exile he was wont to rejoice.

85. And you Novatians cannot deny that you are like him, who, as you say, do not come together to the Church because by penance a hope of return had been given to those who had lapsed. But this is only a pretence, for Novatian contrived his schism through grief at his loss of the Episcopal office.

86. But do you not understand that the Apostle also prophesied of you and says to you: "And ye are puffed up and did not rather mourn, that he who did this deed might be taken away from among you"? He is, then, wholly taken away when his sin is done away, but the Apostle does not say that the sinner is to be shut out of the Church who counsels his cleansing.

CHAPTER XVI.

Comparison between the apostles and Novatians. The fitness of the words, "Ye know not what spirit ye are of," when applied to them. The desire of penance is extinguished by them when they take away its fruit. And thus are sinners deprived of the promises of Christ, though, indeed, they ought not to be too soon admitted to the mysteries. Some examples of repentance.

87. INASMUCH, then, as the Apostle forgave sins, by what authority do you say that they are not to be forgiven? Who has the most reverence for Christ, Paul or Novatian? But Paul knew that the Lord was merciful. He knew that the Lord Jesus was offended more by the harshness of the disciples than by their pitifulness.

88. Furthermore, Jesus rebuked James and John when they spoke of bringing down fire from heaven to consume those who refused to receive the Lord, and said to them: "Ye know not whose spirit ye are of; for the Son of Man is not come to destroy men's lives but to save them." To them, indeed, He said, "Ye know not whose spirit ye are of," who were of His spirit; but to you He says, "Ye are not of My spirit, who hold not fast My clemency, who reject My mercy, who refuse repentance which I willed to be preached by the apostles in My Name."

89. For it is in vain that you say that you preach repentance who remove the fruits of repentance. For men are led to the pursuit of anything either by rewards or results, and every pursuit grows slack by delay. And for this reason the Lord, in order that the devotion of His disciples might be increased, said that everyone who had left all that was his, and followed God, should receive sevenfold more both here and hereafter.

First of all He promised the reward *here*, to do away with the tedium of delay, and again *hereafter*, that we might learn to believe that rewards will also be given to us hereafter. Present rewards are then an earnest of those hereafter.

90. If, then, any one, having committed hidden sins, shall nevertheless diligently do penance, how shall he receive those rewards if not restored to the communion of the Church? I am willing, indeed, that the guilty man should hope for pardon, should seek it with tears and groans, should seek it with the aid of the tears of all the people, should implore forgiveness; and if communion be postponed two or three times, that he should believe that his entreaties have not been urgent enough, that he must increase his tears, must come again even in greater trouble, clasp the feet of the faithful with his arms, kiss them, wash them with tears, and not let them go, so that the Lord Jesus may say of him too: "His sins which are many are forgiven, for he loved much."

91. I have known penitents whose countenance was furrowed with tears, their cheeks worn with constant weeping, who offered their body to be trodden under foot by all, who with faces ever pale and worn with fasting bore about in a yet living body the likeness of death.

CHAPTER XVII.

*That gentleness must be added to severity, as is shown in the case of
St. Paul at Corinth. The man had been baptized, though the
Novatians argue against it. And by the word "destruction" is not
meant annihilation but severe chastening.*

92. WHY do we postpone the time of pardon for those who
have mortified themselves, who during life have done
themselves to death? "Sufficient," says St. Paul, "to such
a one is this punishment which is inflicted by the many;
so that contrariwise, ye should rather forgive him and
comfort him, lest by any means he should be swallowed
up with overmuch sorrow." If the punishment which is
inflicted by the many is sufficient for condemnation, the
intercession which is made by many is also sufficient for
the remission of sin. The Master of morals, Who both
knows our weakness and is the interpreter of the will of
God, wills that comfort should be given, lest sorrow
through the weariness of long delay should swallow up
the penitent.

93. The Apostle then forgave him, and not only forgave
him, but desired that love to him should again grow
strong. He who is loved receives not harshness but mercy.
And not only did he himself forgive him only, but willed
that all should forgive him, and says that he forgave for
the sake of others, lest many should be longer saddened
on account of one. "To whom," says he, "ye have
forgiven anything, I forgive also, for I also have forgiven
for your sakes in the person of Christ, for we are not
ignorant of his devices." Rightly can he be on his guard
against the serpent who is not ignorant of his devices, of
which there are so many to our detriment. He is always

desirous to do harm, always desirous to circumvent us, that he may cause death; but we ought to take heed lest our remedy become an occasion of triumph for him; for we are circumvented by him, if any one perish through overmuch sorrow, who might be set free by pitifulness.

94. And that we may know that this person was baptized, he added: "I wrote to you in my epistle to have no company with fornicators, not altogether with fornicators of this world." And farther on he adds: "But now I write unto you not to keep company if any man that is named a brother be a fornicator, or covetous, or an idolator." Those whom he has joined together under one penalty, he willed to attain together to forgiveness. "If any be such," he says, "with him not to eat." How severe he is with the obstinate, how indulgent to those who seek. Against those rises up in arms the injury done to Christ, whilst the calling upon Christ aids these.

95. But lest anyone be perplexed because it is written: "I have delivered such an one unto Satan for the destruction of the flesh," and should say: How can he attain forgiveness whose whole flesh has perished, seeing that it is evident that man was redeemed both in body and soul, and is saved in both and that neither the soul without the body, nor yet the body without the soul, since both are united by their fellowship in the deeds that have been done, can be without fellowship either in punishment or in reward? Let this suffice for an answer to him: That "destruction" does not mean the complete annihilation of the flesh, but its chastening. For as he who is dead to sin

lives to God, so the allurements of the flesh perish, and the flesh dies to its lusts, in order that it may live again to purity and to other good works.

96. And what more suitable example can we take than one from our common mother? For the earth itself, from which we are all taken, when it is not worked and cultivated, seems to be desert; and the field dies to the vines or olive-trees with which it was planted, and yet it does not lose its own nutritive power, which is, as it were, its life. And then later, when cultivation begins once more, and the seed is sown for which the land seems suitable, it breaks forth again more fruitful than before with its products. It is not, then, anything so strange if our flesh is said to die, and yet is understood to be subdued rather than annihilated.

BOOK II.

CHAPTER I.

St. Ambrose gives additional rules concerning repentance, and shows that it must not be delayed.

1. ALTHOUGH in the former book we have written many things which may tend to the more perfect practice of repentance, yet inasmuch as a great deal more may be added, we will continue the repast so as not to seem to have relinquished the provisions of our teaching only half consumed.

2. For repentance must be taken in hand not only anxiously, but also quickly, lest perchance that father of the house in the Gospel who planted a fig-tree in his vineyard should come and seek fruit on it, and finding none, say to the vine-dresser: "Cut it down, why doth it cumber the ground?" And unless the vine-dresser should intercede and say: "Lord, let it alone this year also, until I dig about it and dung it, and if it bear fruit—well; but if not let it be cut down."

3. Let us then dung this field which we possess, and imitate those hard-working farmers, who are not ashamed to satiate the land with rich dung and to scatter the grimy ashes over the field, that they may gather more abundant crops.

4. And the Apostle teaches us how to dung it, saying: "I count all things but dung, that I may gain Christ," and he, through evil report and good report, attained to pleasing Christ. For he had read that Abraham, when confessing

himself to be but dust and ashes,[3052] in his deep humility found favor with God. He had read how Job, sitting among the ashes, regained all that he had lost. He had heard in the utterance of David, how God "raiseth the poor out of the dust, and lifteth the needy out of the dunghill."

5. Let us then not be ashamed to confess our sins unto the Lord. Shame indeed there is when each makes known his sins, but that shame, as it were, ploughs his land, removes the ever-recurring brambles, prunes the thorns, and gives life to the fruits which he believed were dead. Follow him who, by diligently ploughing his field, sought for eternal fruit: "Being reviled we bless, being persecuted we endure, being defamed we entreat, we are made as the offscouring of the world." If you plough after this fashion you will sow spiritual seed. Plough that you may get rid of sin and gain fruit. He ploughed so as to destroy in himself the last tendency to persecution. What more could Christ give to lead us on to the pursuit of perfection, than to convert and then give us for a teacher one who was a persecutor?

CHAPTER II.

A passage quoted by the heretics against repentance is explained in two ways, the first being that Heb. vi. 4 refers to the impossibility of being baptized again; the second, that what is impossible with man is possible with God.

6. BEING then refuted by the clear example of the Apostle and by his writings, the heretics yet Endeavour to resist further, and say that their opinion is supported by apostolic authority, bringing forward the passage in the Epistle to the Hebrews: "For it is impossible that those who were once enlightened, and have tasted the heavenly gift, and have been made partakers of the Holy Spirit, and have tasted the good word of God, and the powers of the world to come, should if they fall away be again renewed unto repentance, crucifying again the Son of God, and put Him to open shame."

7. Could Paul teach in opposition to his own act? He had at Corinth forgiven sin through penance, how could he himself speak against his own decision? Since, then, he could not destroy what he had built, we must assume that what he says was different from, but not contrary to, what had gone before. For what is contrary is opposed to itself, what is different has ordinarily another meaning. Things which are contrary are not such that one can support the other. Inasmuch, then, as the Apostle spoke of remitting penance, he could not be silent as to those who thought that baptism was to be repeated. And it was right first of all to remove our anxiety, and to let us know that even after baptism, if any sinned their sins could be forgiven them, lest a false belief in a reiterated baptism should lead astray those who were destitute of all hope of forgiveness.

And secondly, it was right to set forth in a well-reasoned argument that baptism is not to be repeated.

8. And that the writer was speaking of baptism is evident from the very words in which it is stated that it is impossible to renew unto repentance those who were fallen, inasmuch as we are renewed by means of the laver of baptism, whereby we are born again, as Paul says himself: "For we are buried with Him through baptism into death, that, like as Christ rose from the dead through the glory of the Father, so we, too, should walk in newness of life." And in another place: "Be ye renewed in the spirit of your mind, and put on the new man which is created after God." And elsewhere again: "Thy youth shall be renewed like the eagle," because the eagle after death is born again from its ashes, as we being dead in sin are through the Sacrament of Baptism born again to God, and created anew. So, then, here as elsewhere, he teaches one baptism. "One faith," he says, "one baptism."

9. This, too, is plain, that in him who is baptized the Son of God is crucified, for our flesh could not do away sin unless it were crucified in Jesus Christ. And then it is written that: "All we who were baptized into Jesus Christ were baptized into His death." And farther on: "If we have been planted in the likeness of His death, we shall be also in the likeness of His resurrection, knowing that our old man was fastened with Him to His cross." And to the Colossians he says: "Buried with Him by baptism, wherein ye also rose again with Him." Which was written to the intent that we should believe that He is crucified in us, that our sins may be purged through Him, that He, Who alone can forgive sins, may nail to His cross the

handwriting which was against us. In us He triumphs over principalities and powers, as it is written of Him: "He made a show of principalities and powers, triumphing over them in Himself."

10. So, then, that which he says in this Epistle to the Hebrews, that it is impossible for those who have fallen to be "renewed unto repentance, crucifying again the Son of God, and putting Him to open shame," must be considered as having reference to baptism, wherein we crucify the Son of God in ourselves, that the world may be by Him crucified for us, who triumph, as it were, when we take to ourselves the likeness of His death, who put to open shame upon His cross principalities and powers, and triumphed over them, that in the likeness of His death we, too, might triumph over the principalities whose yoke we throw off. But Christ was crucified once, and died to sin once, and so there is but one, not several baptisms.

11. But what of the passage wherein the doctrine of baptisms is spoken of? Because under the Law there were many baptisms or washings, he rightly rebukes those who forsake what is perfect and seek again the first principles of the word. He teaches us that the whole of the washings under the Law are done away with, and that there is one baptism in the sacraments of the Church. But he exhorts us that leaving the first principles of the word we should go on to perfection. "And this," he says, "we will do, if God permits," for no one can be perfect without the grace of God.

12. And indeed I might also say to anyone who thought that this passage spoke of repentance, that things which

are impossible with men are possible with God; and God is able whensoever He wills to forgive us our sins, even those which we think cannot be forgiven. And so it is possible for God to give us that which it seems to us impossible to obtain. For it seemed impossible that water should wash away sin, and Naaman the Syrian thought that his leprosy could not be cleansed by water. But that which was impossible God made to be possible, Who gave us so great grace. In like manner it seemed impossible that sins should be forgiven through repentance, but Christ gave this power to His apostles, which has been transmitted to the priestly office. That, then, has become possible which was impossible. But, by a true reasoning, he convinces us that the reiteration by any one of the Sacrament of Baptism is not permitted.

CHAPTER III.

Explanation of the parable of the Prodigal Son, in which St. Ambrose applies it to refute the teaching of the Novatians, proving that reconciliation ought not to be refused to the greatest offender upon suitable proof of repentance.

13. AND the Apostle does not contradict the plain teaching of Christ, Who set forth, as a comparison of a repentant sinner, one going to a foreign country after receiving all his substance from his father, wasted it in riotous living, and later, when feeding upon husks, longed for his father's bread and then gained the robe, the ring, the shoes, and the slaying of the calf, which is a likeness of the Passion of the Lord, whereby we receive forgiveness.

14. Well is it said that he went into a foreign country who is cut off from the sacred altar, for this is to be separated from that Jerusalem which is in heaven, from the citizenship and home of the saints. For which reason the Apostle says: "Therefore now ye are no more strangers and foreigners, but fellow-citizens with the saints and of the household of God."

15. "And," it is said, "wasted his substance." Rightly, for he whose faith halts in bringing forth good works does consume it. For, "faith is the substance of things hoped for, the evidence of things not seen." And faith is a good substance, the inheritance of our hope.

16. And no wonder if he was perishing for hunger, who lacked the divine nourishment, impelled by the want of which he says: "I will arise and go to my father, and will say unto him: Father, I have sinned against heaven, and

before thee." Do you not see it plainly declared to us, that we are urged to prayer for the sake of gaining the sacrament? and do you wish to take away that for the sake of which penance is undertaken? Deprive the pilot of the hope of reaching port, and he will wander uncertainly here and there on the waves. Take away the crown from the athlete, and he will fail and lie on the course. Take from the fisher the power of catching his booty, and he will cease to cast the nets. How, then, can he, who suffers hunger in his soul, pray more earnestly to God, if he has no hope of the heavenly food?

17. "I have sinned," he says, "against heaven, and before thee." He confesses what is clearly a sin unto death, that you may not think that anyone doing penance is rightly shut out from pardon. For he who has sinned against heaven has sinned either against the kingdom of heaven, or against his own soul, which is a sin unto death, and against God, to Whom alone is said: "Against Thee only have I sinned, and done evil before Thee."

18. So quickly does he gain forgiveness, that, as he is coming, and is still a great way off, his father meets him, gives him a kiss, which is the sign of sacred peace; orders the robe to be brought forth, which is the marriage garment, which if anyone have not, he is shut out from the marriage feast; places the ring on his hand, which is the pledge of faith and the seal of the Holy Spirit; orders the shoes to be brought out,[3074] for he who is about to celebrate the Lord's Passover, about to feast on the Lamb, ought to have his feet protected against all attacks of spiritual wild beasts and the bite of the serpent; bids the calf to be slain, for "Christ our Passover hath been

sacrificed." For as often as we receive the Blood of the Lord, we proclaim the death of the Lord. As, then, He was once slain for all, so whensoever forgiveness of sins is granted, we receive the Sacrament of His Body, that through His Blood there may be remission of sins.

19. Therefore most evidently are we bidden by the teaching of the Lord to confer again the grace of the heavenly sacrament on those guilty even of the greatest sins, if they with open confession bear the penance due to their sin.

CHAPTER IV.

St. Ambrose turns against the Novatians themselves another objection concerning blasphemy against the Holy Spirit, showing that it consists in an erroneous belief, proving this by St. Peter's words against Simon Magus, and other passages, exhorting the Novatians to return to the Church, affirming that such is our Lord's mercy that even Judas would have found forgiveness had he repented.

20. But we have heard that you are accustomed to bring forward as an objection that which is written: "Every sin and blasphemy shall be forgiven unto men, but blasphemies against the Spirit shall not be forgiven unto men. And whosoever shall speak a word against the Son of Man, it shall be forgiven him, but whosoever shall speak against the Holy Spirit, it shall not be forgiven him, neither in this world, nor in that which is to come." By which quotation the whole of your assertion is destroyed and done away, for it is written: "Every sin and blasphemy shall be forgiven unto men." Why, then, do you not remit them? Why do you bind chains which you do not loose? Why do you tie knots which you do not unfasten? Forgive the others, and deal with those who you think are bound forever by the authority of the Gospel for sinning against the Holy Spirit.

21. But let us consider the case of those whom the Lord so binds, going back to the words before the passage quoted, that we may understand it more clearly: The Jews were saying: "This man doth not cast out devils, but by Beelzebub, prince of the devils." Jesus replied: "Every kingdom divided against itself shall be destroyed, and every city or house divided against itself shall not stand; for if Satan casteth out Satan, he is divided against himself, how then shall his kingdom stand? But if

I cast out devils by Beelzebub, by whom do your sons cast them out?"

22. Now we see plainly here that the words are expressly used of those who were saying that the Lord Jesus cast out devils through Beelzebub, to whom the Lord gave that answer, because they were of the heritage of Satan, who compared the Savior of all to Satan, and attributed the grace of Christ to the kingdom of the devil. And that we might know that He was speaking of this blasphemy, He added: "O generation of vipers, how can ye speak good, being yourselves evil?" He says, then, that those who thus speak attain not to forgiveness.

23. Then, when Simon, depraved by long practice of magic, had thought he could gain by money the power of conferring the grace of Christ and the infusion of the Holy Spirit, Peter said: "Thou hast neither part nor lot in this faith, for thy heart is not right with God. Repent therefore of this thy wickedness, and pray the Lord, if perchance this thought of thy heart may be forgiven thee, for I see that thou art in the bond of iniquity and in the bitterness of gall." We see that Peter by his apostolic authority condemns him who blasphemes against the Holy Spirit through magic vanity, and all the more because he had not the clear consciousness of faith. And yet he did not exclude him from the hope of forgiveness, for he called him to repentance.

24. The Lord then replies to the blasphemy of the Pharisees, and refuses to them the grace of His power, which consists in the remission of sins, because they asserted that His heavenly power rested on the help of the devil. And He affirms that they act with satanic spirit who

divide the Church of God, so that He includes the heretics and schismatics of all times, to whom He denies forgiveness, for every other sin is concerned with single persons, this is a sin against all. For they alone wish to destroy the grace of Christ who rend asunder the members of the Church for which the Lord Jesus suffered, and the Holy Spirit was given us.

25. Lastly, that we may know that He is speaking of those who destroy the unity of the Church, we find it written: "He that is not with Me is against Me, and he that gathered not with Me, scattereth." And that we might know that He is speaking of these, He at once added: "Therefore I say unto you, every sin and blasphemy shall be forgiven unto men, but blasphemies against the Spirit shall not be forgiven unto men." When He says, "Therefore say I unto you," is it not evident that He intended the words following to be laid to heart by us beyond the others? And He rightly added: "A good tree bringeth forth good fruits, but a bad tree bringeth forth bad fruits," for an evil association cannot produce good fruits. The tree, then, is the association; the fruits of the good tree are the children of the Church.

26. Return, then, to the Church, those of you who have wickedly separated yourselves. For He promises forgiveness to all who are converted, since it is written: "Whosoever shall call on the Name of the Lord shall be saved." And lastly, the Jewish people who said of the Lord Jesus, "He hath a devil," and "He casteth out devils through Beelzebub," and who crucified the Lord Jesus, are, by the preaching of Peter, called to baptism, that they may put away the guilt of so great a wickedness.

27. But what wonder is it if you should deny salvation to others, who reject your own, though they lose nothing who seek for penance from you? For I suppose that even Judas might through the exceeding mercy of God not have been shut out from forgiveness, if he had expressed his sorrow not before the Jews but before Christ. "I have sinned," he said, "in that I have betrayed righteous blood." Their answer was: "What is that to us, see thou to that." What other reply do you give, when one guilty of a smaller sin confesses his deed to you? What do you answer but this: "What is that to us, see thou to that"? The halter followed on those words, but the punishment is all the more severe, the smaller the sin is.

28. But if they be not converted, do you at least repent, who by many a slip have fallen from the lofty pinnacle of innocence and faith. We have a good Lord, Whose will it is to forgive all, Who called you by the prophet, and said: "I, even I, am He that blotteth out transgressions, and I will not remember, but do thou remember, and let us plead together."

CHAPTER V.

As to the words of St. Peter to Simon Magus, from which the Novatians infer that there was no forgiveness for the latter, it is pointed out that St. Peter, knowing his evil heart, might well use words of doubt, and then by some Old Testament instances it is pointed out that "perchance" does not exclude forgiveness. The apostles transmitted to us that penitence, the fruits of which are shown in the case of David. St. Ambrose then adduces the example of the Ephraimites, whose penitence must be followed in order to gain the divine mercy and the sacraments.

29. THE Novatians bring up a question from the words of the Apostle Peter. Because he said, "if perchance," they think that he did not imply that forgiveness would be granted on repentance. But let them consider concerning whom the words were spoken: of Simon, who did not believe through faith, but was meditating trickery. So too the Lord to him who said, "Lord, I will follow Thee withersoever Thou goest," replied, "Foxes have holes." For He knew that the man's sincerity was not wholly perfect. If, then, the Lord refused to him who was not baptized permission to follow Him, because He saw that he was not sincere, do you wonder that the Apostle did not absolve him who after baptism was guilty of deceit, and whom he declared to be still in the bond of iniquity?

30. But let this be my answer to them. As to myself, I say that Peter did not doubt, and I do not think that so great a question can be burked by the questionable interpretation of a single word. For if they think that Peter doubted, did God doubt, Who said to the prophet Jeremiah: "Stand in the court of the Lord's house, and thou shalt give an answer to all Judah, to those who come to worship in the Lord's house, even all the words which I have appointed

for thee to answer them. Keep not back a word, perchance they will hearken and be converted." Let them say, then, that God also knew not what would happen.

31. But ignorance is not implied in that word, but the common custom of holy Scripture is observed, in order to simplicity of utterance. Inasmuch as the Lord says also to Ezekiel: "Son of man, I will send thee unto the house of Israel, to those who have angered Me, both themselves and their fathers, unto this day, and thou shalt say unto them, Thus saith the Lord, if perchance they will hear and be afraid." Did He not know that they could or could not be converted? So, then, that expression is not always a proof of doubt.

32. Lastly, the wise men of this world, who stake all their reputation on expressions and words, do not everywhere use the Latin word *forte*, "perchance," or its Greek equivalent τάχα, as an expression of doubt. And so they say that their earliest poet used the words,
...ἦ ΄ τάχα χήρη
...ἔσομαι,
which is, "I shall soon be a widow;" and the passage goes on:
... τάχα γάρ σε κατακνέουσιν Ἀχαιοὶ
πάντες εφορμηθέντες.

But he had no doubt that when all were joining in the attack one might well be laid low by all.

33. But let us use our own instances rather than foreign ones. You find in the Gospel that the Son Himself says of the Father (when He had sent His servants to His vineyard, and they had been slain), that the Father said, "I

will send My well-beloved Son, perchance they will reverence Him." And in another place the Son says of Himself: "Ye know neither Me nor My Father; for if ye knew Me, ye would perchance know My Father also."

34. If, then, Peter used those words which were used by God without any prejudice to His knowledge, why should we not assume that Peter also used them without prejudice to his belief? For he could not doubt concerning the gift of Christ, Who had given him the power of forgiving sins; especially since he was bound not to leave any place for the craftiness of heretics who desire to deprive men of hope, in order the more easily to insinuate into the despairing their opinion as to the reiteration of baptism.

35. But the apostles, having this baptism according to the direction of Christ, taught repentance, promised forgiveness, and remitted guilt, as David taught when he said: "Blessed are they whose transgressions are forgiven, and whose sins are covered. Blessed is the man to whom the Lord hath not imputed sin." He calls each blessed, both him whose sins are remitted by the font, and him whose sin is covered by good works. For he who repents ought not only to wash away his sin by his tears, but also to cover and hide his former transgressions by amended deeds, that sin may not be imputed to him.

36. Let us, then, cover our falls by our subsequent acts; let us purify ourselves by tears, that the Lord our God may hear us when we lament, as He heard Ephraim when weeping, as it is written: "I have surely heard Ephraim weeping." And He expressly repeats the very words of

Ephraim: "Thou hast chastised me and I was chastised, like a calf I was not trained." For a calf disports itself, and leaves its stall, and so Ephraim was untrained like a calf far away from the stall; because he had forsaken the stall of the Lord, followed Jeroboam, and worshipped the calves, which future event was prophetically indicated through Aaron, namely, that the people of the Jews would fall after this manner. And so repenting, Ephraim says: "Turn Thou me, and I shall be turned, for Thou art the Lord my God. Surely in the end of my captivity I repented, and after I learned I mourned over the days of confusion, and subjected myself to Thee because I received reproach and made Thee known."

37. We see how to repent, with what words and with what acts, that the days of sin are called "days of confusion;" for there is confusion when Christ is denied.

38. Let us, then, submit ourselves to God, and not be subject to sin, and when we ponder the remembrance of our offences, let us blush as though at some disgrace, and not speak of them as a glory to us, as some boast of overcoming modesty, or putting down the feeling of justice. Let our conversion be such, that we who did not know God may now ourselves declare Him to others, that the Lord, moved by such a conversion on our part, may answer to us: "Ephraim is from youth a dear son, a pleasant child, for since My words are concerning him, I will verily remember him, therefore have I hastened to be over him; I will surely have mercy on him, saith the Lord."

39. And what mercy He promises us, the Lord also shows, when He says further on: "I have satiated every thirsty soul, and have satisfied every hungry soul. Therefore, I awaked and beheld, and My sleep was sweet unto Me." We observe that the Lord promises His sacraments to those who sin. Let us, then, all be converted to the Lord.

CHAPTER VI.

St. Ambrose teaches out of the prophet Isaiah what they must do who have fallen. Then referring to our Lord's proverbial expression respecting piping and dancing, he condemns dances. Next by the example of Jeremiah he sets forth the necessary accompaniments of repentance. And lastly, in order to show the efficacy of this medicine of penance, he enumerates the names of many who have used it for themselves or for others.

40. BUT if they be not converted, do you at least repent, who by many a slip have fallen from the lofty pinnacle of innocence and faith. We have a good Lord, Whose will it is to forgive all, Who called you by the prophet and said: "I, even I, am He that blotteth out thy transgressions, and I will not remember, but do thou remember that we may plead together." "I," He says, "will not remember, but do thou remember," that is to say, "I do not recall those transgressions which I have forgiven thee, which are covered, as it were, with oblivion, but do thou remember them. I will not remember them because of My grace, do thou remember them in order to correction; remember, thou mayest know that the sin is forgiven, boast not as though innocent, that thou aggravate not the sin, but thou wilt be justified, confess thy sin." For a shamefaced confession of sins looses the bands of transgression.

41. You see what God requires of you, that you remember that grace which you have received, and boast not as though you had not received it. You see by how complete a promise of remission He draws you to confession. Take heed, lest by resisting the commandments of God you fall into the offence of the Jews, to whom the Lord Jesus said: "We piped to you and ye danced not; we wailed and ye wept not."

42. The words are ordinary words, but the mystery is not ordinary. And so one must be on one's guard, lest, deceived by any common interpretation of this saying, one should suppose that the movements of wanton dances and the madness of the stage were commended; for these are full of evil in youthful age. But the dancing is commended which David practiced before the ark of God. For everything is seemly which is done for religion, so that we need be ashamed of no service which tends to the worship and honoring of Christ.

43. Dancing, then, which is an accompaniment of pleasures and luxury, is not spoken of, but spiritually such as that wherewith one raises the eager body, and suffers not the limbs to lie slothfully on the ground, nor to grow stiff in their accustomed tracks. Paul danced spiritually, when for us he stretched forward, and forgetting the things which were behind, and aiming at those which were before, he pressed on to the prize of Christ. And you, too, when you come to baptism, are warned to raise the hands, and to cause your feet wherewith you ascend to things eternal to be swifter. This dancing accompanies faith, and is the companion of grace.

44. This, then, is the mystery. "We piped to you," singing in truth the song of the New Testament, "and ye danced not." That is, did not raise your souls to the spiritual grace. "We wailed, and ye wept not." That is, ye did not repent. And therefore was the Jewish people forsaken, because it did not repent, and rejected grace. Repentance came by John, grace by Christ. He, as the Lord, gives the one; the other is proclaimed, as it were, by the servant. The Church, then, keeps both that it may both attain to

grace and not cast away repentance, for grace is the gift of One Who confers it; repentance is the remedy of the sinner.

45. Jeremiah knew that penitence was a great remedy, which he in his Lamentations took up for Jerusalem, and brings forward Jerusalem itself as repenting, when he says: "She wept sore in the night, and her tears are on her cheeks, nor is there one to comfort her of all who love her. The ways of Zion do mourn." And he says further: "For these things I weep, my eyes have grown dim with weeping, because he who used to comfort me is gone far from me." We notice that he thought this the bitterest addition to his woes, that he who used to comfort the mourner was gone far from him. How, then, can you take away the very comfort by refusing to repentance the hope of forgiveness?

46. But let those who repent learn how they ought to carry it out, with what zeal, with what affection, with what intention of mind, with what shaking of the inmost bowels, with what conversion of heart: "Behold," he says, "O Lord, that I am in distress, my bowels are troubled by my weeping, my heart is turned within me."

47. Here you recognize the intention of the soul, the faithfulness of the mind, the disposition of the body: "The elders of the daughters of Zion sat," he says, "upon the ground, they put dust upon their heads, they girded themselves with haircloth, the princes hung their heads to the ground, the virgins of Jerusalem fainted with weeping, my eyes grew dim, my bowels were troubled, my glory was poured on the earth."

48. So, too, did the people of Nineveh mourn, and escaped the destruction of their city. Such is the remedial power of repentance, that God seems because of it to change His intention. To escape is, then, in your own power; the Lord wills to be entreated, He wills that men should hope in Him, He wills that supplication should be made to Him. Thou art a man, and willest to be asked to forgive, and dost thou think that God will pardon thee without asking Him?

49. The Lord Himself wept over Jerusalem, that, inasmuch as it would not weep itself, it might obtain forgiveness through the tears of the Lord. He wills that we should weep in order that we may escape, as you find it in the Gospel: "Daughters of Jerusalem, weep not for Me, but weep for yourselves."

50. David wept, and obtained of the divine mercy the removal of the death of the people who were perishing, when of the three things proposed for his choice he selected that in which he might have the most experience of the divine mercy. Why do you blush to weep for your sins, when God commanded even the prophets to weep for the people?

51. And, lastly, Ezekiel was bidden to weep for Jerusalem, and he took the book, at the beginning of which was written: "Lamentation, and melody, and woe," two things sad and one pleasant, for he shall be saved in the future who has wept most in this age. "For the heart of the wise is in the house of mourning, and the heart of fools in the house of feasting." And the Lord Himself said: "Blessed are ye that weep now, for ye shall laugh."

CHAPTER VII.

An exhortation to mourning and confession of sins for Christ is moved by these and the tears of the Church. Illustration from the story of Lazarus. After showing that the Novatians are the successors of those who planned to kill Lazarus, St. Ambrose argues that the full forgiveness of every sin is signified by the odor of the ointment poured by Mary on the feet of Christ; and further, that the Novatian heretics find their likeness in Judas, who grudged and envied when others rejoiced.

52. LET us, then, mourn for a time, that we may rejoice for eternity. Let us fear the Lord, let us anticipate Him with the confession of our sins, let us correct our backslidings and amend our faults, lest of us too it be said: "Woe is me, my soul, for the godly man is perished from the earth, and there is none amongst men to correct them."

53. Why do you fear to confess your sins to our good Lord? "Set them forth," He says, "that thou mayest be justified." The rewards of justification are set before him who is still guilty of sin, for he is justified who voluntarily confesses his own sin; and lastly, "the just man is his own accuser in the beginning of his speaking." The Lord knows all things, but He waits for your words, not that He may punish, but that He may pardon. It is not His will that the devil should triumph over you and accuse you when you conceal your sins. Be beforehand with your accuser: if you accuse yourself, you will fear no accuser; if you report yourself, though you were dead you shall live.

54. Christ will come to your grave, and if He finds there weeping for you Martha the woman of good service, and Mary who carefully heard the Word of God, like holy Church which has chosen the best part, He will be moved

with compassion, when at your death He shall see the tears of many and will say: "Where have ye laid him?" that is to say, in what condition of guilt is he? in which rank of penitents? I would see him for whom ye weep, that he himself may move Me with his tears. I will see if he is already dead to that sin for which forgiveness is entreated.

55. The people will say to Him, "Come and see." What is the meaning of "Come"? It means, Let forgiveness of sins come, let the life of the departed come, the resurrection of the dead, let Thy kingdom come to this sinner also.

56. He will come and will command that the stone be taken away which his fall has laid on the shoulders of the sinner. He could have removed the stone by a word of command, for even inanimate nature is wont to obey the bidding of Christ. He could by the silent power of His working have removed the stone of the sepulchre, at Whose Passion the stones being suddenly removed many sepulchres of the dead were opened, but He bade men remove the stone, in very truth indeed, that the unbelieving might believe what they saw, and see the dead rising again, but in a type that He might give us the power of lightening the burden of sins, the heavy pressure as it were upon the guilty. Ours it is to remove the burdens, His to raise again, His to bring forth from the tombs those set free from their bands.

57. So the Lord Jesus, seeing the heavy burden of the sinner, weeps, for the Church alone He suffers not to weep. He has compassion with His beloved, and says to him that is dead, "Come forth," that is, Thou who liest in

darkness of conscience, and in the squalor of thy sins, as in the prison-house of the guilty, come forth, declare thy sins that thou mayest be justified. "For with the mouth confession is made unto salvation."

58. If you have confessed at the call of Christ the bars will be broken, and every chain loosed, even the stench of the bodily corruption be grievous. For he had been dead four days and his flesh stank in the tomb; but He Whose flesh saw no corruption was three days in the sepulchre, for He knew no evils of the flesh, which consists of the substances of the four elements. However great, then, the stench of the dead body may be, it is all done away so soon as the sacred ointment has shed its odor; and the dead rises again, and the command is given to loose his hands who till now was in sin; the covering is taken from his face which veiled the truth of the grace which he had received. But since he has received forgiveness, the command is given to uncover his face, to lay bare his features. For he whose sin is forgiven has nothing whereof to be ashamed.

59. But in the presence of such grace given by the Lord, of such a miracle of divine bounty, when all ought to have rejoiced, the wicked were stirred up and gathered a council against Christ, and wished moreover to kill Lazarus also. Do you not recognize that you are the successors of those whose hardness you inherit? For you too are angry and gather a council against the Church, because you see the dead come to life again in the Church, and to be raised again by receiving forgiveness of their sins. And thus, so far as in you, you desire to slay again through envy those who are raised to life.

60. But Jesus does not revoke His benefits, nay, rather He amplifies them by additions of His liberality, He anxiously revisits him who was raised again, and rejoicing in the gift of the restored life, He comes to the feast which His Church has prepared for Him, at which he who had been dead is found as one amongst those sitting down with Christ.

61. Then all wonder who look upon him with the pure gaze of the mind, who are free from envy, for such children the Church has. They wonder, as I said, how he who yesterday and the day before lay in the tomb is one of those sitting with the Lord Jesus.

62. Mary herself pours ointment on the feet of the Lord Jesus. Perchance for this reason on His feet, because one of the lowliest has been snatched from death, for we are all the body of Christ, but others perchance are the more honorable members. The Apostle was the mouth of Christ, for he said, "Ye seek a proof of Christ that speaketh in me." The prophets through whom He spake of things to come were His mouth, would that I might be found worthy to be His foot, and may Mary pour on me her precious ointment, and anoint me and wipe away my sin.

63. What, then, we read concerning Lazarus we ought to believe of every sinner who is converted, who, though he may have been stinking, nevertheless is cleansed by the precious ointment of faith. For faith has such grace that there where the dead stank the day before, now the whole house is filled with good odor.

64. The house of Corinth stank, when it was written concerning it: "It is reported that there is fornication among you, and such fornication as is not even among the Gentiles." There was a stench, for a little leaven had corrupted the whole lump. A good odor began when it was said: "If ye forgive anything to any one I forgive also. For what I also have forgiven, for your sakes have I done it in the person of Christ." And so, the sinner being set free, there was great joy in that place, and the whole house was filled with the odor of the sweetness of grace. Wherefore the Apostle, knowing well that he had shed upon all the ointment of apostolic forgiveness, says: "We are a sweet savour of Christ unto God in them that are saved."

65. At the pouring forth, then, of this ointment all rejoice; Judas alone speaks against it. So, too, now he who is a sinner speaks against it, he who is a traitor blames it, but he is himself blamed by Christ, as he knows not the remedy of the Lord's death, and understands not the mystery of that so great burial. For the Lord both suffered and died that He might redeem us from death. This is manifest from the most excellent value from His death, which is sufficient for the absolution of the sinner, and his restoration to fresh grace; so that all may come and wonder at his sitting at table with Christ, and may praise God, saying: "Let us eat and feast, for he was dead and is alive again, had perished and is found." But any one devoid of faith objects: "Why does He eat with publicans and sinners?" This is his answer: "They that are whole have no need of the physician, but they that are sick."

CHAPTER VIII.

In urging repentance St. Ambrose turns to his own case, expressing the wish that he could wash our Lord's feet like the woman in the Gospel, which is a great pattern of penitence, though such as cannot attain to it find acceptance. He prays for himself, especially that he may sorrow with sinners, who are better than himself. Those for whom Christ died are not to be contemned.

66. Show, then, your wound to the Physician that He may heal it. Though you show it not, He knows it, but waits to hear your voice. Do away your scars by tears. Thus did that woman in the Gospel, and wiped out the stench of her sin; thus did she wash away her fault, when washing the feet of Jesus with her tears.

67. Would that Thou, Lord Jesus, mightest reserve for me the washing off from Thy feet of the stains contracted since Thou walkest in me! O that Thou mightest offer to me to cleanse the pollution which I by my deeds have caused on Thy steps! But whence can I obtain living water, wherewith I may wash Thy feet? If I have no water I have tears, and whilst with them I wash Thy feet I trust to cleanse myself. Whence is it that Thou shouldst say to me: "His sins which are many are forgiven, because he loved much"? I confess that I owe more, and that more has been forgiven me who have been called to the priesthood from the tumult and strife of the law courts and the dread of public administration; and therefore I fear that I may be found ungrateful, if I, to whom more has been forgiven, love less.

68. But all are not able to equal that woman, who was deservedly preferred even to Simon, who was giving the feast to the Lord; who gave a lesson to all who desire to

gain forgiveness, by kissing the feet of Christ, washing them with her tears, wiping them with her hair, and anointing them with ointment.

69. In a kiss is the sign of love, and therefore the Lord Jesus says: "Let her kiss Me with the kisses of her mouth." What is the meaning of the hair, but that you may learn that, having laid aside all the pomp of worldly trappings, you must implore pardon, throw yourself on the earth with tears, and prostrate on the ground move pity. In the ointment, too, is set forth the savour of a good conversation. David was a king, yet he said: "Every night will I wash my bed, I will water my couch with tears." And therefore he obtained such a favor, as that of his house the Virgin should be chosen, who by her child-bearing should bring forth Christ for us. Therefore is this woman also praised in the Gospel.

70. Nevertheless if we are unable to equal her, the Lord Jesus knows also how to aid the weak, when there is no one who can prepare the feast, or bring the ointment, or carry with her a spring of living water. He comes Himself to the sepulchre.

71. Would that Thou wouldst vouchsafe to come to this sepulchre of mine, O Lord Jesus, that Thou wouldst wash me with Thy tears, since in my hardened eyes I possess not such tears as to be able to wash away my offence. If Thou shalt weep for me I shall be saved; if I am worthy of Thy tears I shall cleanse the stench of all my offences; if I am worthy that Thou weep but a little, Thou wilt call me out of the tomb of this body and will say: "Come forth," that my meditations may not be kept pent up in the

narrow limits of this body, but may go forth to Christ, and move in the light, that I may think no more on works of darkness but on works of light. For he who thinks on sins endeavors to shut himself up within his own consciousness.

72. Call forth, then, Thy servant. Although bound with the chain of my sins I have my feet fastened and my hands tied; being now buried in dead thoughts and works, yet at Thy call I shall go forth free, and shall be found one of those sitting at Thy feast, and Thy house shall be filled with precious ointment. If Thou hast vouchsafed to redeem any one, Thou wilt preserve him. For it shall be said, "See, he was not brought up in the bosom of the Church, nor trained from childhood, but hurried from the judgment-seat, brought away from the vanities of this world, growing accustomed to the singing of the choir instead of the shout of the crier, but he continues in the priesthood not by his own strength, but by the grace of Christ, and sits among the guests at the heavenly table.

73. Preserve, O Lord, Thy work, guard the gift which Thou hast given even to him who shrank from it. For I knew that I was not worthy to be called a bishop, because I had devoted myself to this world, but by Thy grace I am what I am. And I am indeed the least of all bishops, and the lowest in merit; yet since I too have undertaken some labor for Thy holy Church, watch over this fruit, and let not him whom when lost Thou didst call to the priesthood, to be lost when a priest. And first grant that I may know how with inmost affection to mourn with those who sin; for this is a very great virtue, since it is written: "And thou shalt not rejoice over the children of Judah in

the day of their destruction, and speak not proudly in the day of their trouble." Grant that so often as the sin of anyone who has fallen is made known to me I may suffer with him, and not chide him proudly, but mourn and weep, so that weeping over another I may mourn for myself, saying, "Tamar hath been more righteous than I."

74. Perchance a maiden may have fallen, deceived and hurried away by those occasions which are the sources of sins. Well, we who are older sin, too. In us, too, the law of this flesh wars against the law of our mind, and makes us captives of sin, so that we do what we would not. Her youth is an excuse for her, I now have none, for she ought to learn, we ought to teach. So that "Tamar hath been more righteous than I."

75. We inveigh against some one's covetousness, let us call to mind whether we ourselves have never done anything covetously; and if we have, since covetousness is the root of all evils, and is working in our bodies like a serpent secretly under the earth, let each of us say: "Tamar hath been more righteous than I."

76. If we have been seriously moved against any one, a layman may act hastily for a smaller matter than a bishop. Let us ponder that with ourselves and say, He who is reproved for quick temper is more righteous than I. For if we thus speak, we guard ourselves against this, that the Lord Jesus or one of His disciples should say to us: "Thou beholdest the mote in thy brother's eye, but beholdest not the beam which is in thine own eye. Thou hypocrite, cast out first the beam out of thine own eye, and then shalt thou see to cast out the mote out of thy brother's eye."

77. Let us, then, not be ashamed to say that our fault is more serious than that of him whom we think we must reprove, for this is what Judah did who reprimanded Tamar, and remembering his own fault said: "Tamar is more righteous than I." In which saying there is a deep mystery and a moral precept; and therefore is his offence not reckoned to him, because he accused himself before he was accused by others.

78. Let us, then, not rejoice over the sin of any one, but rather let us mourn, for it is written: "Rejoice not against me, O my enemy, because I have fallen, for I shall arise; for if I sit in darkness the Lord shall be a light unto me, I will bear the indignation of the Lord, because I have sinned against Him, until He maintain my cause, and execute judgment for me, and bring me forth to the light, and I shall behold His righteousness. Mine enemy, too, shall see it and shall be covered with confusion, which said unto me, Where is the Lord thy God? Mine eyes shall behold her, and she shall be for treading down as the mire in the streets." And this not unreservedly, for he who rejoices at the fall of another rejoices at the victory of the devil. Let us, then, rather mourn when we hear that one has perished for whom Christ died, Who despises not even the straw in time of harvest.

79. O that He may not cast away this straw at His harvest, the empty stalks of my produce; but may He gather it in, as is said by some one: "Woe is me, for I am become as one that gathereth straw in harvest, and grape gleanings in the vintage," that He may eat of the firstfruits at least of His grace in me, though He approve not the later fruit.

CHAPTER IX.

In what way faith is necessary for repentance. Means for paying our debts, in which work, prayer, tears, and fasting are of more value than money. Some instances are adduced, and St. Ambrose declares that generosity is profitable, but only when joined with faith; it is, moreover, liable to certain defects. He goes on to speak of some defects in repentance, such as too great haste in seeking reconciliation, considering abstinence from sacraments all that is needed, of committing sin in hope of repenting later.

80. So, then, it is fitting for us to believe both that sinners must repent and that forgiveness is to be given on repentance, yet still as hoping for forgiveness as granted upon faith, not as a debt, for it is one thing to earn, and another presumptuously to claim a right. Faith asks for forgiveness, as it were, by covenant, but presumption is more akin to demand than to request. Pay first that which you owe, that you may be in a position to ask for what you have hoped. Come with the disposition of an honest debtor, that you may not contract a fresh liability, but may pay that which is due of the existing debt with the possessions of your faith.

81. He who owes a debt to God has more help towards payment than he who is indebted to man. Man requires money for money, and this is not always at the debtor's command. God demands the affection of the heart, which is in our own power. No one who owes a debt to God is poor, except one who has made himself poor. And even if he have nothing to sell, yet has he wherewith to pay. Prayer, fasting, and tears are the resources of an honest debtor, and much more abundant than if one from the price of his estate offered money without faith.

82. Ananias was poor, when after selling his land he brought the money to the apostles, and was not able with it to pay his debt, but involved himself the more. That widow was rich who cast her two small pieces into the treasury, of whom Christ said: "This poor widow hath cast in more than they all." For God requires not money but faith.

83. And I do not deny that sins may be diminished by liberal gifts to the poor, but only if faith commend what is spent. For what would the giving of one's whole property benefit without charity?

84. There are some who aim at the credit of generosity for pride alone, because they wish thereby to gain the good opinion of the multitude for leaving nothing to themselves; but whilst they are seeking rewards in this life, they are laying up none for the life to come, and having received their reward here they cannot hope for it there.

85. Some again, having, through impulsive excitement and not after long consideration, given their possessions to the Church, think that they can claim them back. These gain neither the first nor the second reward, for the gift was made thoughtlessly, its recall sacrilegiously.

86. Some repent of having distributed their property to the poor. But they who are doing penance must not repent of this, lest they repent of their own repentance. For many seek for penance through fear of future punishment, being conscious of their sins, and having received their penance are held back by fear of the public entreaties. These

persons seem to have sought for repentance for their evil deeds, but to exercise it for their good ones.

87. Some seek penance because they wish to be at once restored to communion. These wish not so much to loose themselves as to bind the priest, for they do not put off the guilt from their own conscience, but lay it on that of the priest, to whom the command is given: "Give not that which is holy to the dogs, neither cast your pearls before the swine;" that is to say, that partaking of the holy Communion is not to be allowed to those polluted with impurity.

88. And so one may see those walking in other attire, who ought to be weeping and groaning because they had defiled the robe of sanctification and grace; and women loading their ears with pearls, and weighing down their necks, who had better have bent to Christ than to gold, and who ought to be weeping for themselves, because they have lost the pearl from heaven.

89. There are, again, some who think that it is penitence to abstain from the heavenly sacraments. These are too cruel judges of themselves, who prescribe a penalty for themselves but refuse the remedy, who ought to be mourning over their self-imposed penalty, because it deprives them of heavenly grace.

90. Others think that license is granted them to sin, because the hope of penitence is before them, whereas penitence is the remedy, not an incentive to sin. For the salve is necessary for the wound, not the wound for the salve, since a salve is sought because of the wound, the

wound is not wished for on account of the salve. The hope which is put off to a future season is but feeble, for every season is uncertain, and hope does not outlive all time.

CHAPTER X.

In order to do away with the feeling of shame which holds back the guilty from public penance, St. Ambrose points out the advantage of prayers offered by the whole Church, and sets forth the example of saints who have sorrowed. Then, after reproving those who imagine that penance may be often repeated, he points out the difficulty of repentance, and how it is to be carried out.

91. CAN any one endure that you should blush to entreat God, when you do not blush to entreat a man? That you should be ashamed to entreat Him Who knows you fully, when you are not ashamed to confess your sins to a man who knows you not? Do you shrink from witnesses and sympathizers in your prayers, when, if you have to satisfy a man, you must visit many and entreat them to be kind enough to intervene; when you throw yourself at a man's knees, kiss his feet, bring your children, still unconscious of guilt, to entreat also for their father's pardon? And you disdain to do this in the Church in order to entreat God, in order to gain for yourself the support of the holy congregation; where there is no cause for shame, except indeed not to confess, since we are all sinners, amongst whom he is the most praiseworthy who is the most humble; he is the most just who feels himself the lowest.

92. Let the Church, our Mother, weep for you, and wash away your guilt with her tears; let Christ see you mourning and say, "Blessed are ye that are sad, for ye shall rejoice." It pleases Him that many should entreat for one. In the Gospel, too, moved by the widow's tears, because many were weeping for her, He raised her son. He heard Peter more quickly when He raised Dorcas, because the poor were mourning over the death of the woman. He also forthwith forgave Peter, for he wept most

bitterly. And if you weep bitterly Christ will look upon you and your guilt shall leave you. For the application of pain does away with the enjoyment of the wickedness and the delight of the sin. And so while mourning over our past sins we shut the door against fresh ones, and from the condemnation of our guilt there arises as it were a training in innocence.

93. Let, then, nothing call you away from penitence, for this you have in common with the saints, and would that such sorrowing for sin as that of the saints were copied by you. David, as it were, "ate ashes for bread, and mingled his drink with weeping," and therefore now rejoices the more because he wept the more: "Mine eyes ran down," he said, "with rivers of water."

94. John wept sore, and, as he tells us, the mysteries of Christ were revealed to him. But that woman who, when she was in sin and ought to have wept, nevertheless rejoiced, and covered herself with a robe of purple and scarlet, and adorned herself with much gold and precious stones, now mourns the misery of eternal weeping.

95. Deservedly are they blamed who think that they often do penance, for they are wanton against Christ. For if they went through their penance in truth, they would not think that it could be repeated again; for as there is but one baptism, so there is but one course of penance, so far as the outward practice goes, for we must repent of our daily faults, but this latter has to do with lighter faults, the former with such as are graver.

96. But I have more easily found such as had preserved their innocence than such as had fittingly repented. Does

anyone think that that is penitence where there still exists the striving after earthly honors, where wine flows, and even conjugal connection takes place? The world must be renounced; less sleep must be indulged in than nature demands; it must be broken by groans, interrupted by sighs, put aside by prayers; the mode of life must be such that we die to the usual habits of life. Let the man deny himself and be wholly changed, as in the fable they relate of a certain youth, who left his home because of his love for a harlot, and, having subdued his love, returned; then one day meeting his old favorite and not speaking to her, she, being surprised and supposing that he had not recognized her, said, when they met again, "It is I." "But," was his answer, "I am not the former I."

97. Well then did the Lord say: "If any man will come after Me, let him deny himself, and take up his cross and follow Me." For they who are dead and buried in Christ ought not again to make their conclusions as though living in the world. "Touch not," it is said, "nor attend to those things which tend to corruption by their very use, for the very customs of this life corrupt integrity."

CHAPTER XI.

The possibility of repentance is a reason why baptism should not be deferred to old age, a practice which is against the will of God in holy Scripture. But it is of no use to practice penance whilst still serving lusts. These must be first subdued.

98. GOOD, then, is penitence, and if there were no place for it, everyone would defer the grace of cleansing by baptism to old age. And a sufficient reason is that it is better, to have a robe to mend, than none to put on; but as that which has been repaired once is restored, so that which is frequently mended is destroyed.

99. And the Lord has given a sufficient warning to those who put off repentance, when He says: "Repent ye, for the kingdom of heaven is at hand." We know not at what hour the thief will come, we know not whether our soul may be required of us this next night. God cast Adam out of Paradise immediately after his fault; there was no delay. At once the fallen were severed from all their enjoyments that they might do penance; at once God clothed them with garments of skins, not of silk.

100. And what reason is there for putting off? Is it that you may sin yet more? Then because God is good you are evil, and "despise the riches of His goodness and long-suffering." But the goodness of the Lord ought rather to draw you to repentance. Wherefore holy David says to all: "Come, let us worship and fall down before Him, and mourn before our Lord Who made us." But for a sinner who has died without repentance, because nothing remains but to mourn grievously and to weep, you find him groaning and saying: "O my son Absalom! my son

Absalom!" For him who is wholly dead mourning is without alleviation.

101. But of those who as exiles and banished from their ancestral homes, which the holy law of Moses had assigned them, will be entangled in the errors of the world, you hear him saying: "By the waters of Babylon we sat down and wept, when we remembered Zion." He sets forth the wailings of those who have fallen, and shows that they who are living in this condition of passing time and changing circumstances ought to repent, after the example of those who, as a reward for sin, had been led into miserable captivity.

102. But nothing causes such exceeding grief as when any one, lying under the captivity of sin, calls to mind whence he has fallen, because he turned aside to carnal and earthly things, instead of directing his mind in the beautiful ways of the knowledge of God.

103. So you find Adam concealing himself, when he knew that God was present, and wishing to be hidden when called by God with that voice which wounded the soul of him who was hiding: "Adam, where art thou?"[3152] That is to say, Wherefore hidest thou thyself? Why art thou concealed? Why dost thou avoid Him, Whom thou once didst long to see? A guilty conscience is so burdensome that it punishes itself without a judge, and wishes for covering, and yet is bare before God.

104. And so no one in a state of sin ought to claim a right to or the use of the sacraments, for it is written: "Thou hast sinned, be still." As David says in the Psalm lately

quoted: "We hanged our harps upon the willows in the midst thereof;" and again: "How shall we sing the Lord's song in a strange land?" For if the flesh wars against the mind, and is not subject to the guidance of the Spirit, that is a strange land which is not subdued by the toil of the cultivator, and so cannot produce the fruits of charity, patience, and peace. It is better, then, to be still when you cannot practice the works of repentance, lest in the very acts of repentance there be that which afterward will need further repentance. For if it be once entered upon and not rightly carried out, it obtains not the result of a first repentance and takes away the use of a later one.

105. When, then, the flesh resists, the soul must be intent upon God, and if results do not follow, let not faith fail. And if the enticements of the flesh come upon us, or the powers of the enemy attack us, let the soul keep in submission to God. For we are then specially oppressed when the flesh yields. And some there are who trouble heavily the wretched soul, seeking to deprive it of all protection. To which case the words apply: "Rase it, rase it, even to the foundations."

106. And David, pitying her, says: "O wretched daughter of Babylon." Wretched indeed, as being the daughter of Babylon, when she ceased to be the daughter of Jerusalem. And yet he calls for a healer for her, and says: "Blessed is he who shall take thy little ones and dash them against the rock."3159 That is to say, shall dash all corrupt and filthy thoughts against Christ, Who by His fear and His rebuke will break down all motions against reason, so as, if anyone is seized by an adulterous love, to extinguish the fire, that he may by his zeal put away the love of a harlot, and deny himself that he may gain Christ.

107. We have then learned that we must do penance, and this at a time when the heat of luxury and sin is giving way; and that we, when under the dominion of sin, must show ourselves Godfearing by refraining, rather than allowing ourselves in evil practices. For if it is said to Moses when he was desiring to draw nearer: "Put off thy shoes from off thy feet," how much more must we free the feet of our soul from the bonds of the body, and clear our steps from all connection with this world.

NOTE ON THE PENITENTIAL DISCIPLINE OF THE EARLY CHURCH.

It was always believed in the Church that the power of binding and loosing had been entrusted by our Lord to His apostles, and by them handed on to their successors in the ministry. The earlier practice would seem to have been short and simple: exclusion from Communion, some outward discipline, not always continued for a long period, and reconciliation on true repentance, these matters being decided by the bishop at his discretion. Gradually the practice became more systematized, various periods of discipline were prescribed for various sins, and the time for this discipline was lengthened.

There were three parts in the discipline of Penitence as a whole:

1. Confession, ἐξομολόγησις, a term used frequently of the whole course.
2. Penance, properly so called, i.e. the mortifications, fasting, etc., prescribed.
3. Reconciliation, performed solemnly by the bishop, often at Easter.

The confession was probably in private to the bishop, who determined whether any public confession should be made or not. But as only great sins—at first, idolatry, adultery, and murder (*peccata mortalia*)—were punished by outward penance, it was clear that the sin must have been very grievous.

The Montanists taught that the Church had not power to forgive great sins, and this led to clearing the doctrine, and from the middle of the third century, even those who had lapsed into idolatry were admitted to penance.

Hermas already says: τοῖς δούλοις τοῦθεοῦ μέτανοιά ἐστι μία, *Mand.* iv. 1. And this rule seems to have been maintained as regards the formal penance and reconciliation, not as implying doubt of possible forgiveness, but as a matter of discipline, and this rule deprived those who fell a second time from communion at least till their deathbed.

For this public penance the Greek words are μετάνοια and ἐξομολόγησις; the Latin, *penitentia* and frequently *exomologesis.* As the word *penitentia* includes not merely sorrow for sin and change of heart, but also penance, or the penalty inflicted by authority, and is used in such phrases as *penitentiam agere* or *facere*, it has been necessary in the translation of the *De Penitentia* to vary the English terms, and to use sometimes repentance, sometimes penance.

For further information on this subject, the reader is referred specially to the Articles, Buss-Disciplin, in the *Freiburg Kirchen-Lexikon*, by Wetzer and Welte; and to those on Exomologesis, Penitence, and Reconciliation, in the *Dict. of Christian Antiquities*, where other authorities and references will be found.

Made in the USA
Middletown, DE
21 April 2022

64472333R00076